Science, She Loves Me

Science, She Loves Me

Edited by Mary Anne Moser, Foreword by Jay Ingram

The Banff Centre

BANFF CENTRE PRESS

Library and Archives Canada Cataloguing in Publication

Science, she loves me / edited by Mary Anne Moser.

Includes index.
ISBN 978-1-894773-37-9

1. Science. I. Moser, Mary Anne

Q171.S34 2011   500   C2011-901605-2

Editor: Janice Zawerbny
Designer: Grace Cheong, www.gracecheong.com
Cover Image: Andrea Juan

The Banff Centre Press
Box 1020, 107 Tunnel Mountain Drive
Banff, Alberta Canada T1L 1H5
www.banffcentre.ca/press/

The Banff Centre
BANFF CENTRE PRESS

Printed in Canada by Friesens

MIX
Paper from responsible sources
FSC
www.fsc.org
FSC® C016245

Contents

To pantheism

Foreword

Jay Ingram

"Science she loves me"? I sure hope so. Where would I be without her? I've been pursuing her for years, trying to grasp her subtler moves, basking in the occasional piece of enlightenment she affords me—a little flush of pleasure at knowing some new, small but cool thing about nature. Yes, science tosses me the odd bone.

Sometimes, I'm sad to admit, I'm tempted to feel a little smug because I know her better than others. But those moments pass quickly when I realize that there are so many who are actually intimate with science, who spend their days engaged in her practice. In that sense, I am more of an arm's-length admirer, although I'd say in my defence that I do admire her from many angles, not just one, and that might just give me a privileged view. Turn it around: there is no doubt that I love science. You get regular "aha" moments, acquire a deeper understanding of the world and the universe, make connections between seemingly disparate things, and prove again and again that humanity, while it has its own glories, is but a tiny part of the whole. I've never been troubled by that claim that science somehow explains away the beauty of nature, the "unweaving of the rainbow" of which Keats accused Newton. Newton himself didn't devote much of his time to the artistic realm, but the grandeur of his work, the picture he painted of the forces of the cosmos, was surely more deserving of admiration, and even artistic imaginings, than criticism.

But how might science love me in return? That is a little tougher. I admit the title caught me by surprise twice: once when I found out that science is a she, and then, more disconcertingly, when I found out that she loves me. I mean, I know her well—I have already admitted to loving her—but I didn't expect it to be reciprocated.

So what about science being a she? Other than the fact that the field has always been male dominated, there isn't an obvious reason why the word should be feminized. I tried flipping it around: Science, He Loves Me. That sounded a little menacing, like a message on a recruitment poster; a guy in a white coat stabbing his finger at you.

You might think that science needs no gender at all, and in fact, giving science a personality runs directly counter to the notion of science as the objective, data-driven analysis of what surrounds us.[1] That is the science the textbooks present. And they are right, in their limited way: science is indeed the pursuit of knowledge grounded in the design of experiments and the generation of data, and even the questions it asks of nature cannot be vague, or general, or wild-eyed. They are crafted to yield answers, and, to be frank, answers that can be published in the journals. So there's a certain mechanistic feel to the scientific process.

But that isn't the way it feels to scientists. They are not unemotional, robotic generators of data. They are not solely dependent on the left side of their brains. Many of them are absolutely crazy about their science, and experience the same highs and lows as any creative person. Yes, there is that difference: they have to be able to defend their results, usually in a numerical, statistical sense, in the community of their peers.

That process does not limit creativity, but it appears to. In public, scientists are often cautious, choosing their words carefully, taking care not to claim too much for their work, knowing that it must stand the test of time and replication. They speak to their colleagues, not to the outside world. And so many of us who live outside that boundary search in vain for the passion that we suspect must be there, but is not evident.

But it must be expressed, and since we cannot expect all scientists to step forward to declare that love, we need the kinds of people who have contributed to this book. They feel the passion, they know that there is more to the equation than numbers, and moreover, they know, as I do, that this "loving science" business is a lifelong pursuit.

---

1 There is no such hesitation about Nature though. Nature is a *she*. Again, substituting Father Nature for Mother Nature doesn't work. The feminine nature of Earth is an ancient tradition based on fertility, birth, and creation, and shows no sign of falling out of favour—see James Lovelock's Gaia.

Science, He Loves Me

Mary Anne Moser

In my family, we did not fling around words like "love." My parents were caring but decidedly unsentimental. And yet here is this word—one that should be used only with great care—in the title of this book. It might make scientists uncomfortable. There is generally not an abundance of emotional expressiveness in the domain. Science, by definition, is an objective pursuit, and there is ample pressure in the science environment to stay cool and accurate when writing about it.

This is a bit of deceit though. There is a lot of passion in science, and in communicating about it. This is a book about that passion. It is about science where you least expect it—in your heart—and about how it finds its way into all kinds of cultural expression. You will find examples here of ways that science is taken up in musical composition, poetry, theatre, or coffee shops. You will see how science evokes emotion—making people laugh, act, explore, or compete. You will see how some of the most engaging examples of science communication ignore the instructive approach that so often confuses science communication with science education.

It is not necessary to treat science like an unappealing but good-for-you topic. Science is a world of the most fascinating ideas and the most novel of discoveries— "the greatest adventure story on Earth," as Brian Greene says. And yet much of the practice around science communications has been concerned with different ways to candy coat difficult scientific ideas, or to translate scientific concepts into lay terms. This is important in certain situations where education is the goal, but it is not the point of the examples in this book. Here we celebrate the culture and communications—from artworks to essays—that take up science because it is part of a personal adventure that people want to share. Understanding how the world is put together is a fascinating pursuit in and of itself, and there are stories to tell! Sometimes these stories are about discoveries, sometimes they are about people, sometimes they are about the awe of the universe, or our love for the planet. Science can delight you or cure you, alarm you, scare you, infuriate you, or just plain bowl you over. There are emotions all around and in the scientific enterprise—ostensibly not in the process itself, but certainly in all of the ways that human beings are involved with it. That is what this book is about—the ways that the passion of both scientists and science communicators makes for riveting experiences with science.

Ask scientists why they became one and they will tell you about personal and emotional experiences that drew them toward science. For science communicators, there is that very same kind of inspiration—a visceral awe at what we can learn from science and what it can help us become, as individuals and as a society. We are, as science shows us, social organisms in a complex ecosystem. People who feel the wonder of this fact in their very cells want to move audiences and enthrall people with the marvels of the world known through science or enabled by engineering.

I am sure this is why I was drawn into the world of science.

My best friend's mother thought we would be derelict in our duties as children if we encountered a dead frog and did not dissect it: "Aren't you dying to see how it's put together?" she'd almost yell, as though it were immoral to play in the woods without knowing how all of nature worked, inside and out. I don't know how many stay-at-home mothers in the 1970s had wax-filled dissecting trays at the ready, but she did, and it opened up a tremendously alluring world for me.

"I don't know how many stay-at-home mothers in the 1970s had wax-filled dissecting trays at the ready, but she did, and it opened up a tremendously alluring world for me."

In the decades that followed, this all-absorbing childhood friendship and fascination with nature led to studying science and then working in research communications, where my natural curiosity was doused, crushed, stifled, discouraged, and all but extinguished by the requirements of the job—the protocols, funding announcements, press releases, backgrounders. I stood at the back of the hall during one of these funding announcements and wondered why it was that we science communicators in universities and funding agencies, sitting on some of the most intrinsically interesting content in the entire world, were too inhibited to share it enthusiastically. I decided I was not going to bore myself, or others, anymore.

Funding announcements may be boring for reasons that have nothing to do with the science, but they are a good example of the communications problems that hinder public engagement with active research. These announcements tell the public about an area of research that we as a society evidently value, but the science itself is difficult to crack and make relevant to lay audiences. How do you get people excited about highly technical and narrow advances in a massive knowledge system?

Science centres deserve a medal here. They take very creative and engaging approaches to science, and more recently have been building relationships with active researchers. But they are not the hothouses of contemporary science and engineering research, so there are limits to what they can access.

It is in universities and research institutions where discoveries are being made, and where people are dedicating their lives to the adventures of new knowledge. The research system in these environments, however, has not traditionally rewarded communications. It takes a passionate scientist or engineer to voluntarily take part in public engagement projects, especially time-consuming projects with large audiences. It takes valuable time away from the career they chose—research. However, since expectations around communications and outreach are now sometimes attached to research funding, the culture is slowly changing. Leaders in science are stepping up to the communications role. The shift is subtle, because strides are constrained: doing too much public engagement or communications work can create turbulence for the science leader within his or her own intellectual community. It is almost as if the science community believes that the science itself will be compromised by the time spent popularizing it—the Carl Sagan Effect, this is sometimes called. In reality, many high-achieving research teams prove this is not the case.

I like to think that the increased willingness of scientists and engineers to communicate publicly about their work is due in part to the maturity of the field of science communications. It is unfortunate that many scientists can tell stories about the way their work has been poorly conveyed in the media and how this may have embarrassed them. Now, every university has staff members trained in science communication, often journalists with science backgrounds who understand and can work with confidence in both worlds. It is getting more and more common to see people with science Ph.D.s join the profession of communications. The growing ranks of well-educated communicators are bringing strong communication skills, years of experience, and a passion for science to the job. And they are helping practising scientists do the outreach work that they are obliged to undertake as publicly funded researchers. Where science journalists may be waning in numbers, at least in the traditional media, the professional staff at post-secondary institutions and other research organizations are growing—and getting creative. There are mammoth science festivals, millions of people watching science on TV, creative public programs, podcasts, blogs, and many new ways of thinking about audiences and students.

Bigger does not mean better though. We are also seeing more energy being put into engagement, the personal connection. Sometimes it's inadvertent. I was never more moved than by the intimacy of the Shanghai Natural History Museum. My visit was a trip back in time. The lobby was empty and quiet, lined with dark benches polished by the uniforms of thousands of long-gone school children. Once-proud cabinets of curiosity were now just very old display cases, floor to ceiling, containing stuffed giraffes (yes, real fur), creatures in formaldehyde, and crudely crafted

RIGHT The Museum of Natural History, unlike most of Shanghai's architecturally contemporary museums, touches a heartstring. It appears to be stuck in time, creaking with old-fashioned dark wood, stuffed mammals, pickled invertebrates, and almost child-like displays using crinkled cellophane and plastic. I was all but alone in the musty building, with its colonially grand entry, and old-fashioned public toilets (involving a river that runs through the adjoined stalls) that I had seen nowhere else in modern Shanghai—and it was a genuine delight. The last line of the Concluding Remarks at the Shanghai Museum of Natural History reads like an apology in light of the other museums now in the city: "As we are limited in time, ability and financial capacity, this exhibition might have many shortcomings. Therefore, we will be very grateful to those who will give us good opinions."

displays. Blue cellophane represented the water around a papier mâché shark. I could feel the sincerity, and the lack of funds. Just before the exit, a plaque pleaded with the visitor to understand the constraints and limited budget. I connected so strongly to this poignant human endeavour.

Then I crossed the river to the new Shanghai Science and Technology Museum, a $180 million project, larger than life on every scale. Humans seemed out of place in this grand facility. It was, perhaps, meant to take you into the future. Walls of electronics were open for business. There was floor upon floor of themed exhibits. Visitors could act in and record their own television show. There was even a 4-D movie theatre! If you had only one museum to visit, though, I would suggest you go to the Natural History Museum. There, the experience was more personally vivid. You would marvel at how scientific ideas have changed over time and feel a connection to the individual scientists and communicators who put these displays together.

I tell you this story because it illustrates what this book means to capture—the personal connection that is possible with science in all kinds of unexpected ways.

This is a book about courageous ways of talking about science. The individual texts and images make up a miscellany that is meant to be dynamic and exploratory. As a whole, it is a collection about cultural activities that tangle with science, from individual sketches to blockbuster films. Individually, these activities take up science with heart and soul and open up a way to look at science as an intriguingly personal pursuit. Each essay offers a view that should be thought-provoking for those interested in science communications today, and each is introduced with an explanation of why it is included in this collection. The essays are organized loosely along a gradient, beginning with the most intimate form of media (Stephen King calls writing a form of telepathy) and ending with the highly mediated blockbuster-movie experience. We start in the world of science, with scientists writing on science in society, and kick things off with a classic: Richard Feynman on the value of science. The book then moves from scientists to science writers, and from science writers to artists who take up science. They are all involved in one-on-one conversations with audiences—whether on a page, in a gallery, on the street, on stage, or in a café. The examples then open up to look at projects that embrace audiences with an added degree of mediation—the Internet, televisions, large-scale spectacles, and contests. The collection ends, not surprisingly, in Hollywood. The mass media can create intimate conversations too, so the gradient is not pure, but this is a miscellany after

LEFT The new Shanghai Science and Technology Museum is modern, technological and interactive.

Respect the audience

Research the audience

Engage the audience

Seduce the audience

Surprise

Connect personally

Care

Keep it simple

Do a lot with a little

Be approachable

Research, research, research

Be accurate

Be ethical

Be extravagant

Invest energy

Evoke emotion

Communicate viscerally

Reveal the unexpected

Use constraints creatively

Think visually

Aesthetics count

Beauty counts

Be culturally relevant

Be funny

Be playful

Be theatrical

Trust your instincts

Test your effectiveness

Tell a story

Become your audience

RIGHT This "manifesto" was co-authored by participants in the inaugural Banff Science Communications program in 2007.

all. In between articles and lists, there are comics and recipes—spicy examples that help to make a point: that science can be such a pleasure. Mix yourself a molecularly inspired cocktail, and enjoy.

A number of the contributors to this volume are associated with the Banff Science Communications program, an annual two-week immersive residency program at The Banff Centre dedicated to creativity in science communications. While there, participants drop any preconceptions we may have about science and communications, set aside for a moment the daily demands of our jobs, and think about what science communication looks like when you put the audience first. You would be surprised to see the creativity explode when engagement is the top priority. It gets personal very quickly.

We live in a world where much is competing for our attention. This is the context for excellence in science communications today. It is therefore a challenge to show and talk about creative science communications in a traditional book format. This book is a two-dimensional attempt to get you thinking about the audiences for science in every dimension. It's a call to get creative with science, and to be inspired by the examples herein. You might just love working with science in this way and the science might just love you back. And that, in case you are wondering, is how love got into the title of this book.

This is Richard P. Feynman's eloquent tribute to the awesomeness—literally—of science and the responsibility that comes with being a scientist. It even includes a poem. Feynman (1918–88) received the Nobel Prize in Physics in 1965. He was a keen popularizer of physics in books and lectures, most certainly a polymath, and his wide-ranging interests did not appear to diminish his esteem in the scientific community.

The Value of Science

Richard P. Feynman

From time to time people suggest to me that scientists ought to give more consideration to social problems—especially that they should be more responsible in considering the impact of science on society. It seems to be generally believed that if the scientists would only look at these very difficult social problems and not spend so much time fooling with less vital scientific ones, great success would come of it.

It seems to me that we *do* think about these problems from time to time, but we don't put a full-time effort into them—the reasons being that we know we don't have any magic formula for solving social problems, that social problems are very much harder than scientific ones, and that we usually don't get anywhere when we do think about them.

I believe that a scientist looking at non-scientific problems is just as dumb as the next guy—and when he talks about a non-scientific matter, he sounds as naive as anyone untrained in the matter. Since the question of the value of science is *not* a scientific subject, this talk is dedicated to proving my point—by example.

The first way in which science is of value is familiar to everyone. It is that scientific knowledge enables us to do all kinds of things and to make all kinds of things. Of course if we make *good* things, it is not only to the credit of science; it is also to the credit of the moral choice which led us to good work. Scientific knowledge is an enabling power to do either good or bad—but it does not carry instructions on how to use it. Such power has evident value—even though the power may be negated by what one does with it.

I learned a way of expressing this common human problem on a trip to Honolulu. In a Buddhist temple there, the man in charge explained a little bit about the Buddhist religion for tourists, and then ended his talk by telling them he had something to say to them that they would *never* forget—and I have never forgotten it. It was a proverb of the Buddhist religion:

To every man is given the key to the gates of heaven; the same key opens the gates of hell.

What then, is the value of the key to heaven? It is true that if we lack clear instructions that enable us to determine which is the gate to heaven and which the gate to hell, the key may be a dangerous object to use.

But the key obviously has value: how can we enter heaven without it?

Instructions would be of no value without the key. So it is evident that, in spite of the fact that it could produce enormous horror in the world, science is of value because it *can* produce *something*.

Another value of science is the fun called intellectual enjoyment which some people get from reading and learning and thinking about it, and which others get from working in it. This is an important point, one which is not considered enough by those who tell us it is our social responsibility to reflect on the impact of science on society.

Is this mere personal enjoyment of value to society as a whole? No! But it is also a responsibility to consider the aim of society itself. Is it to arrange matters so that people can enjoy things? If so, then the enjoyment of science is as important as anything else.

But I would like *not* to underestimate the value of the world view which is the result of scientific effort. We have been led to imagine all sorts of things infinitely more marvellous than the imaginings of poets and dreamers of the past. It shows that the imagination of nature is far, far greater than the imagination of man. For instance, how much more remarkable it is for us all to be stuck—half of us upside down—by a mysterious attraction to a spinning ball that has been swinging in space for billions of years than to be carried on the back of an elephant supported on a tortoise swimming in a bottomless sea.

> "... the imagination of nature is far, far greater than the imagination of man."

I have thought about these things so many times alone that I hope you will excuse me if I remind you of this type of thought that I am sure many of you have had, which no one could ever have had in the past because people then didn't have the information we have about the world today.

For instance, I stand at the seashore, alone, and start to think.

There are the rushing waves
mountains of molecules
each stupidly minding its own business
trillions apart
yet forming white surf in unison.

Ages on ages
before any eyes could see
year after year
thunderously pounding the shore as now.
For whom, for what?

On a dead planet
with no life to entertain.

Never at rest
tortured by energy
wasted prodigiously by the sun
poured into space.
A mite makes the sea roar.

Deep in the sea
all molecules repeat
the patterns of one another
till complex new ones are formed.
They make others like themselves
and a new dance starts.
Growing in size and complexity
living things
masses of atoms
DNA, protein
dancing a pattern ever more intricate.

Out of the cradle
onto dry land
here it is
standing:
atoms with consciousness;
matter with curiosity.

Stands at the sea,
wonders at wondering: I
a universe of atoms
an atom in the universe.

The same thrill, the same awe and mystery, comes again and again when we look at any question deeply enough. With more knowledge comes a deeper, more wonderful mystery, luring one on to penetrate deeper still. Never concerned that the answer may prove disappointing, with pleasure and confidence we turn over each new stone to find unimagined strangeness leading on to more wonderful questions and mysteries—certainly a grand adventure!

It is true that few unscientific people have this particular type of religious experience. Our poets do not write about it; our artists do not try to portray this remarkable thing. I don't know why. Is no one inspired by our present picture of the universe? This value of science remains unsung by singers: you are reduced to hearing not a song or poem, but an evening lecture about it. This is not yet a scientific age.

Perhaps one of the reasons for this silence is that you have to know how to read the music. For instance, the scientific article may say, "The radioactive phosphorus content of the cerebrum of the rat decreases to one-half in a period of two weeks." Now what does that mean?

It means that phosphorus that is in the brain of a rat—and also in mine, and yours—is not the same phosphorus as it was two weeks ago. It means the atoms that are in the brain are being replaced: the ones that were there before have gone away.

So what is this mind of ours: what are these atoms with consciousness? Last week's potatoes! They now can *remember* what was going on in my mind a year ago—a mind which has long ago been replaced.

To note that the thing I call my individuality is only a pattern or dance, *that is* what it means when one discovers how long it takes for the atoms of the brain to be replaced by other atoms. The atoms come into my brain, dance a dance, and then go out—there are always new atoms, but always doing the same dance, remembering what the dance was yesterday.

"The scientist has a lot of experience with ignorance and doubt and uncertainty, and this experience is of very great importance, I think."

When we read about this in the newspaper, it says "Scientists say this discovery may have importance in the search for a cure for cancer." The paper is only interested in the use of the idea, not the idea itself. Hardly anyone can understand the importance of an idea, it is so remarkable. Except that, possibly, some children catch on. And when a child catches on to an idea like that, we have a scientist. It is too late for them to get the spirit when they are in our universities, so we must attempt to explain these ideas to children.

I would now like to turn to a third value that science has. It is a little less direct, but not much. The scientist has a lot of experience with ignorance and doubt and uncertainty, and this experience is of very great importance, I think. When a scientist doesn't know the answer to a problem, he is ignorant. When he has a hunch as to what the result is, he is uncertain. And when he is pretty darn sure of what the result is going to be, he is still in some doubt. We have found it of paramount importance that in order to progress we must recognize our ignorance and leave room for doubt. Scientific knowledge is a body of statements of varying degrees of certainty—some most unsure, some nearly sure, but none *absolutely* certain.

Now, we scientists are used to this, and we take it for granted that it is perfectly consistent to be unsure, that it is possible to live and *not* know. But I don't know whether everyone realizes this is true. Our freedom to doubt was born out of a struggle against authority in the early days of science. It was a very deep and strong struggle: permit us to question—to doubt—to not be sure. I think that it is important that we do not forget this struggle and thus perhaps lose what we have gained. Herein lies a responsibility to society.

We are all sad when we think of the wondrous potentialities human beings seem to have, as contrasted with their small accomplishments. Again and again people have thought that we could do much better. Those of the past saw in the nightmare of their times a dream for the future. We, of *their* future, see that their dreams, in certain ways surpassed, have in many ways remained dreams. The hopes for the future today are, in good share, those of yesterday.

It was once thought that the possibilities people had were not developed because most of the people were ignorant. With universal education, could all men be Voltaires? Bad can be taught at least as efficiently as good. Education is a strong force, but for either good or evil.

Communications between nations must promote understanding—so went another dream. But the machines of communication can be manipulated. What is communicated can be truth or lie. Communication is a strong force, but also for either good or evil.

The applied sciences should free men of material problems at least. Medicine controls diseases. And the record here seems all to the good. Yet there are some patiently working today to create great plagues and poisons for use in warfare tomorrow.

Nearly everyone dislikes war. Our dream today is peace. In peace, man can develop best the enormous possibilities he seems to have. But maybe future men will find that peace, too, can be good and bad. Perhaps peaceful men will drink out of boredom. Then perhaps drink will become the great problem, which seems to keep man from getting all he thinks he should out of his abilities.

Clearly, peace is a great force—as are sobriety, material power, communication, education, honesty, and the ideals of many dreamers. We have more of these forces to control than did the ancients. And maybe we are doing a little better than most of them could do. But what we ought to be able to do seems gigantic compared with our confused accomplishments.

Why is this? Why can't we conquer ourselves?

Because we find that even great forces and abilities do not seem to carry with them clear instructions on how to use them. As an example, the great accumulation of understanding as to how the physical world behaves only convinces one that this behaviour seems to have a kind of meaninglessness. The sciences do not directly teach good and bad.

Through all ages of our past, people have tried to fathom the meaning of life. They have realized that if some direction or meaning could be given to our actions, great human forces would be unleashed. So, very many answers have been given to the question of the meaning of it all. But the answers have been of all different sorts, and the proponents of one answer have looked with horror at the actions of the believers in another—horror, because from a disagreeing point of view all the great potentialities of the race are channelled into a false and confining blind alley. In fact, it is from the history of the enormous monstrosities created by false belief that philosophers have realized the apparently infinite and wondrous capacities of human beings. The dream is to find the open channel.

What, then, is the meaning of it all? What can we say to dispel the mystery of existence?

If we take everything into account—not only what the ancients knew, but all of what we know today that they didn't know—then I think we must frankly admit that *we do not know*.

But, in admitting this, we have probably found the open channel.

This is not a new idea; this is the idea of the age of reason. This is the philosophy that guided the men who made the democracy that we live under. The idea that no one really knew how to run a government led to the idea that we should arrange a system by which new ideas could be developed, tried out, and tossed out if necessary, with more new ideas brought in—a trial-and-error system. This method was a result of the fact that science was already showing itself to be a successful venture at the end of the eighteenth century. Even then it was clear to socially minded people that the openness of possibilities was an opportunity, and that doubt and discussion were essential to progress into the unknown. If we want to solve a problem that we have never solved before, we must leave the door to the unknown ajar.

"If we want to solve a problem that we have never solved before, we must leave the door to the unknown ajar."

We are at the very beginning of time for the human race. It is not unreasonable that we grapple with problems. But there are tens of thousands of years in the future. Our responsibility is to do what we can, learn what we can, improve the solutions, and pass them on. It is our responsibility to leave the people of the future a free hand. In the impetuous youth of humanity, we can make grave errors that can stunt our growth for a long time. This we will do if we say we have the answers now, so young and ignorant as we are. If we suppress all discussion, all criticism, proclaiming "This is the answer, my friends; man is saved!" we will doom humanity for a long time to the chains of authority, confined to the limits of our present imagination. It has been done so many times before.

It is our responsibility as scientists, knowing the great progress which comes from a satisfactory philosophy of ignorance, the great progress which is the fruit of freedom of thought, to proclaim the value of this freedom; to teach how doubt is not to be feared but welcomed and discussed; and to demand this freedom as our duty to all coming generations.

Like Richard Feynman, Lawrence M. Krauss does not think that scientists are uniquely wise guides for shaping public policy, but argues that scientists need to work harder to keep science in cultural and governance debates. Krauss is one of the few scientists who is also considered a public intellectual. He is an active defender of reason rather than religion in government, and is a frequent contributor to the New York Times. He is a professor in the physics department and director of the Origins Initiative at Arizona State University, and the author of several best-selling books, including The Physics of Star Trek.

Unlikely Bedfellows:
Science and Politics in the Modern World

Lawrence M. Krauss

"We live in a world which is penetrated through and through by science, and which is both whole and real. We cannot turn it into a game simply by taking sides."—Jacob Bronowski, *Science and Human Values*, 1956

Scientists have no special knowledge that makes them wise guides for public policy, nor should they be allocated a special role in decision-making when it comes to public-policy issues. But, as the scientist-humanist Jacob Bronowski so cogently stated, science should play a central role. After all, there is not a single major policy issue confronting our modern society that does not have science or technology at its basis, from climate change to energy production, from the economy to national security.

Scientists have a responsibility, especially because most of us are supported by the public purse, to be prepared to assist policy-makers and the public more broadly by providing clear access to information that can help inform the public debate. This is particularly important in the current climate, where not only is scientific illiteracy so rampant, but there are cultural, political, and religious factors that mitigate against the proper use of empirical knowledge.

Several years ago I had one of those "aha" experiences, the kind of thing that puts in clear context a notion that might be playing in the back of your head. A friend brought me back a ten-pound note from a trip to England. On the back was a picture of Charles Darwin. I then pulled a U.S. one-dollar bill out my wallet and looked at the back. I found a picture of a pyramid with an eye on it!

The comparison, while tongue-in-cheek, nevertheless makes a point. Whether or not the great eye on the back of the U.S. dollar represents the Eye of Providence, dating back to Egyptian mythology, or, as some have suggested, a Freemason conspiracy by the country's founding fathers, the dichotomy between the two images reflects a remarkable cognitive dissonance.

On the one hand, the U.S. is among the most technologically advanced countries in the world. On the other hand, deeply rooted cultural challenges persist that tend to marginalize, distort, and sometimes openly threaten the proper and vital relationship that should exist between science, culture, and governance. If scientists abdicate their responsibilities to help illuminate the nature of physical reality and the consequences of actions based on myth or censorship, our very democratic system can be imperiled.

This dissonance is not unique to the U.S.; it occurs to greater or lesser degrees in the rest of the developed world. Moreover, science has recently, and often, become hostage to politics—precisely when we need sound science as the basis of public policy more than ever. Consider, for example, the changes that took place in the U.S. over the past twenty years.

In 1990, then-President George H. W. Bush, in a speech to the National Academy of Sciences said:

> Science, like any field of endeavor, relies on freedom of inquiry; and one of the hallmarks of that freedom is objectivity. Now more than ever, on issues ranging from climate change to AIDS research to genetic engineering to food additives, government relies on the impartial perspective of science for guidance.[1]

This is a marvellous description of the proper role of science in the political arena, and should be contrasted with a statement from a member of the latter President Bush's administration slightly more than a decade later. In 2003, White House press secretary Scott McClellan said, "This administration looks at the facts, and reviews the best available science *based on what's right for the American people* (italics mine)."[2]

It is not hard to sense the not-so-subtle shift in perception, or its dangerous implications. As Jacob Bronowski warned in 1956:

> The world today is made, it is powered by science; and for any man to abdicate an interest in science is to walk with open eyes towards slavery.[3]

In the case of the last Bush administration in the U.S., on issues ranging from national security to climate change, from energy production to environmental protection, we witnessed how policies based on censoring or distorting scientific information can undermine our economic and political stability.

But perhaps the biggest disappointment associated with McClellan's statement is how far it diverges from the ethos of science itself. As Richard Feynman said:

> The only way to have real success in science … is to describe the evidence very carefully without regard to the way you feel it should be. If you have a theory, you must try and explain what's good about it and what's bad about it equally. In science you learn a sort of standard integrity and honesty.[4]

There are some who claim that science somehow distorts our moral compass, and that a religious framework is required for public policy to truly guide society to improve the human condition. Many of these are the same people who see threats in the teaching of evolution, for example, which they believe undermines the divine nature of what they perceive to be the human soul. But Feynman's quote makes it clear that science can lead to an ethical world, a world where reason and rationality help uncover the data vital to the kind of sound decision-making that forms the basis of sound public policy.

"If scientists abdicate their responsibilities to help illuminate the nature of physical reality and the consequences of actions based on myth or censorship, our very democratic system can be imperiled."

Moreover, science may not merely feed the soul. In the twenty-first century, it will be essential for feeding our bellies as well. Studies in the U.S., for example, suggest that investments in science and technology have produced annualized societal returns that range from 20 to 67 percent. Moreover, about half the nations's growth in GDP per capita during the last half-century can be attributed to scientific and engineering achievements.

Yet in spite of the clear importance of science for our economic welfare in particular and for informing public policy decisions more generally, little attention is paid. During the last U.S. presidential election, both presidential candidates were offered three different options for debates or forums on science and technology issues; both opted instead to participate on forums on faith. The public didn't seem to mind.

There are numerous reasons for politicians to flock to faith over science. In the first place, faith is a motherhood issue. Claiming to be a person of faith is virtually bulletproof. Unlike certain religious groups, for example, atheists do not vote as a block, nor do they vote against believers. If they did, there would be no one for whom to vote.

But there is another challenge here. Politics, at its basis, often relies less on reason than it does on a priori belief, much as conventional faith does. People react viscerally to politicians, and often vote as their parents voted, just as they often adopt their parents' faith. As long as both topics go beyond issues that can be settled by evidence or lack of evidence, there is little room left for reason. Like it or not, such irrationality is a central part of what it means to be a human. All of us probably need to believe six impossible things before breakfast each day in order to get up and go to work. These may range from the trivial—you look great in the mirror; you didn't really make a fool of yourself at the party the night before—to the more serious—your dead-end job is actually fulfilling; the woman down the hall whom you cannot get out of your mind feels the same way about you. For most people, religion and politics are ways to make sense of what they perceive to be an irrational world, a world that is not fair, a world in which human justice is an afterthought.

The public's apparent lack of interest in the scientific literacy of our politicians does not mean that scientific questions are actually irrelevant to the general public, however. Popular ambivalence may rather reflect the fact that many adults are simply scientifically illiterate. A 2006 National Science Foundation survey found that 25 percent of Americans did not know the Earth goes around the sun, for example.[5] The statistics about knowledge of scientific facts are not significantly different in the U.S. from elsewhere, except in the case of creationism. There, 60 percent of U.S. adults surveyed in 2007 stated their belief that God created humans in their present form fewer than ten thousand years ago, in spite of the fact that we have direct historical evidence of human society and culture extending back well before this time.

Scientific illiteracy is not confined to the poorly educated; it reaches into our cultural and intellectual elites, where ignorance of science is often considered a badge of distinction. But the effects of this illiteracy are most pernicious in the media, where, due to a lack of comfort on scientific matters, many journalists hesitate to make pronouncements on even the most cut-and-dry issues, from evolution to energy.

"... the great virtue of science is that most often one side is demonstrably wrong. The discovery of which side is which is precisely how we progress."

Most journalists are trained to always seek two sides to every story. However, the great virtue of science is that most often one side is demonstrably wrong. The discovery of which side is which is precisely how we progress. Independent of journalistic fairness, the effort to always find dissenters to any issue with scientific consensus is disingenuous. One can always find a Ph.D. to support an argument, even for a flat Earth. On issues like global warming or evolution, simply presenting one statement by a scientist and one statement by a fringe dissenter gives the uninformed public the misperception that there may be a controversy, when in fact none exists at all.

All of this poses a challenge for those, like myself, who believe that the blurring of distinctions between science, nonscience, and nonsense represents one of the greatest threats to our peace and security, and to the very health of our democracy.

Several years before Bronowski, Einstein warned, in response to the first use of nuclear weapons in war: "Everything has changed, save the way we think." Sixty years later we face new and unprecedented global societal challenges in the twenty-first century, from climate change to energy crises, from nuclear proliferation to economic sustainability. Each will require decision-makers and the people they represent to face empirical realities in an honest way. Business as usual—abdicating an interest, in Bronowski's language—cannot continue with impunity.

The lack of clear scientific thinking has perhaps been most obvious in the preparation of public policy on the issue of nuclear missiles and missile defence. On March 23, 1983, President Ronald Reagan called upon "the scientific community in our country, those who gave us nuclear weapons, to turn their great talents to the cause of mankind and world peace; to give us a means of rendering these nuclear weapons impotent and obsolete."[6]

This sounds laudable, but the physics of missile defence has not changed since 1972, when the scientific community convinced President Richard Nixon that the idea of building a missile-defence system was so flawed and destabilizing that it was worth, instead, signing an Anti-Ballistic Missile Treaty with the Soviet Union.

The flawed physics behind missile defence is simple to explain. In the first place, the most expensive nuclear warhead to build is the very first one. Once the appropriate technology has been developed, nuclear weapons are relatively cheap—the biggest bang for your buck, as my friends in Los Alamos say. But a missile-interceptor system is incredibly expensive.

Now consider the following: If one builds a missile-defence system that is 90 percent efficient—far better than anything that has been developed in the real world—an enemy need only launch five missiles instead of one in order to have a fifty-fifty chance of penetrating this system. If you are a country bent on committing national suicide by launching a ballistic nuclear weapon against the U.S. or any of its allies, and you currently have ten missiles, just build forty more. Better still, if you launch just a single missile containing one armed warhead, and ten decoys—say aluminum balloons with a similar profile—the chance of penetrating a system that cannot distinguish weapons from decoys jumps to 80 percent per missile.

The net effect, therefore, of building a missile-defence system is to convince your enemies to build more, not fewer weapons—that is if you have a workable missile-defence system in the first place, which America does not. While never actually tested against an incoming missile with decoys, U.S. test interceptors failed to hit their targets at least 40 percent of the time, even when the inceptors knew exactly where the targets were coming from, and when they would be launched—a luxury we would not be likely to have in a real combat situation.

But the Pentagon was faced with a dilemma. In 2003, administration officials testified before Congress that interceptors capable of shooting down enemy missiles with a 90 percent efficiency would be in place by September 2004, in time for President Bush to challenge his enemies: "You fire. We will shoot it down!"

What do you do in such a situation, where the empirical data and the claims diverge to such a degree? The simple solution was to stop testing the system before it was to be deployed, at a cost of $60 billion. (It turns out that in 2002, 50 percent

34

of Americans polled thought the U.S. already had a missile-defence system in place; it would have been a lot cheaper to simply keep it that way. The distinction between illusion and reality would have been no less.)

The other aspects of current nuclear-defence strategy are equally depressing. There exist perhaps ten thousand nuclear warheads in the U.S., with at least a thousand on hair-trigger alert, more than enough to destroy the civilized world several times over. All of this without a single credible threat! Moreover, under the Nuclear Non-Proliferation Treaty that is so colouring current dealings with Iran, nuclear nations like the U.S. are committed to reducing their arsenals, something they have taken no major steps toward in recent times.

Einstein's remarks of sixty years ago unfortunately continue to ring true. That we have survived thus far, with nonsense in the place of sound policy on an issue that could affect our future more than any other, is nothing short of miraculous.

During an administration that is hostile to science, and to evidence-based decision-making, such as we experienced in the U.S. during the eight years of George W. Bush's presidency, scientists needed to work from the outside. This is what occurred when sixty leading scientists, including an unprecedented number of Nobel laureates and National Medal of Science winners, wrote a public letter to the president urging a restoration of scientific integrity in public policy-making. Now, with an administration that is much more receptive, we need to support sensible initiatives. If necessary, some of us need to volunteer for a role in government—one that will help address the very issues about which we have expressed concern.

"As a civilization, scientific ideas are among the most remarkable leaps of the human intellect, leaps worth preserving and celebrating."

We owe it to the next generation to take ownership of issues like nuclear proliferation and global warming. There is reason for optimism with the election of Barack Obama, who has populated his administration with distinguished scientists and who has promised to restore scientific integrity in Washington.

Moreover, in spite of the ambivalence reflected in some polls, there is an innate popular understanding that science and technology will be essential to meet the challenges we face as a society. When reports began to surface warning that the avian flu might become a threat to humans, for example, everyone from the president down called for studies to determine how quickly the virus might mutate from birds to human beings. No one suggested that "intelligent design," for example, could provide answers.

Ultimately, the reason we need to keep science as an integral part of our society is neither economic nor technological, but cultural. As a civilization, scientific ideas are among the most remarkable leaps of the human intellect, leaps worth preserving and celebrating. This, in large part, is what drives my own activism. I find it tragic that more people are not in a position to experience the awe and wonder that the universe can and should provide. To be scientifically illiterate is to be illiterate, to miss out on some of what is best about being human. To quote Robert Wilson, the first head of the Fermi National Accelerator Laboratory (a large particle accelerator near Chicago), who was asked by Congress whether the mammoth machine would aid our national defence: "No, but it will help keep our nation worth defending!"

1 Remarks to the National Academy of Sciences, April 23, 1990.

2 Christopher Marquis, "Bush Misuses Science Data, Report Says," *New York Times*, August 8, 2003.

3 Jacob Bronowski, *Science and Human Values* (New York: Julian Messner, Inc., 1956).

4 Richard P. Feynman as told to Ralph Leighton, *What Do You Care What Other People Think? Further Adventures of a Curious Character* (New York: WW Norton, 1988).

5 National Science Indicators 2006, 2007. National Science Foundation, Division of Science Resources Statistics, Arlington, VA.

6 This remark was added to an otherwise routine speech at the White House in support of the defence budget.

So, a physicist walks into a bar ....

Sometimes the work of scientists touches on profound topics—the nature of the cosmos, the origins of consciousness, the price of freedom. These are all good bar-stool topics. At other times, science is more straightforward. Maybe you just want to know what on this woozy Earth is alcohol, anyway. John Swain is an experimental high-energy physicist (with a strong interest in related theory) at Northeastern University in Boston. He is also a frequent contributor to texts and broadcasts aimed at general audiences. Here, he shows us what good science writing can look like, and shares his passion for the research and theory that make him a scientist first. Pull up a stool—there's a recipe for a mixed drink at the end, with a twist of science.

Proof? I'll Give You Proof!

John Swain

Alcohol, in the words of one of the great philosophers of our time, can be "the cause of, and solution to, all of life's problems." Those were the words of Homer (well, Simpson, but it's still a pretty good quotation!) and perhaps summarize best the remarkably intense and yet ambiguous nature of this substance.

I should say at the outset, in an attempt to be responsible, that this isn't supposed to be an essay glorifying alcohol abuse. I'll freely admit to liking a few drinks now and then, but I've also seen a friend die from alcoholism and it's not nice, so please do keep that in mind!

That said, what exactly is the big deal about this simple molecule, and what interesting things could we be led to as we think about it? Actually, all of science is connected, and anything can be a window into everything! An outrageous claim? You want proof? I'll give you proof—in more than one way! So put your beer goggles on, and off we go!

In the interests of clarity, let's start with a definition: The term "alcohol" actually refers to any substance with an −OH (oxygen and hydrogen) bound to a carbon atom (which in turn will have bonds to other things—that factor that distinguishes one alcohol from another). Unless one says otherwise, alcohol usually means "ethyl alcohol" or "ethanol," in which the carbon atom in question is attached to two others in a chain, and hydrogen atoms are attached wherever there's a space left—five in all.

It comes as a surprise to many that even the strictest teetotaller manufactures, as part of the daily business of being alive, a decent fraction of a standard drink's worth of ethanol each day. This is actually quite natural, since we clearly have the biochemical apparatus required to metabolize even relatively large quantities of the stuff. But where did alcohol itself come from originally? The story is interesting and linked to nothing less than the evolution of life itself!

Flash back about four billion years to the Earth in its earlier days—the Earth was a relatively oxygen-free place. Relatively simple metabolic processes like the ones that let yeast turn sugar into alcohol held sway, cells divided without limit as long as there was food, and nothing really complicated could get going. Oxygen was a deadly poison.

The story of the rise of oxygen levels though history is a long and fascinating one, which neither time nor space really allow us to go into in detail here. The point is simply that the higher levels of oxygen enabled new and wonderful things to happen! Ozone (three atoms of oxygen joined together) formed, protecting the surface of the planet, and, in particular, land, from ultraviolet radiation. The energy released from oxidative reactions enabled new forms of complex life to emerge, and with this new protection from radiation, life could move out of the seas. Eventually the oxygen concentration settled at around 20 percent—a good thing, since at less than 15 percent there would be no fires and at over 25 percent, fires would likely spread uncontrollably, even with damp vegetation for fuel!

The emergence of oxygen-based metabolism enabled dramatically more complex organisms to form, but it also required a co-operation and restraint in growth that had not been realized with the older "fermentative" metabolism. In fact, it required more than restraint; cells had to be willing to die for the good of an organism as a whole—a process called "apoptosis."

Despite the new developments, complex organisms didn't entirely forget how to do fermentation! Every time you run for too long and find yourself panting away after you've stopped, you are taking advantage of the old ways. You can actually access fermentative metabolism to run your muscles, and pay off the "oxygen debt" afterwards to undo the products of fermentative metabolism. In the case of the overexerted jogger, fermentation doesn't result in alcohol but in lactic acid, and it's the buildup of that that can give you muscle cramps. A similar fermentative process, but now involving micro-organisms, produces the lactic acid that gives sauerkraut its bite and, as you might have guessed from the name, helps to turn milk into yogurt.

Before we return to the sort of fermentation that makes alcohol and all the wonderful things it does, let's consider a fascinating and little-known theory put forth by Albert Szent-Györgyi, the brilliant Hungarian biochemist who discovered vitamin C. He suggested that at least some cancers could be due to cells "forgetting" that they should use the modern, oxygen-driven, "let's all pull together for the good of the whole complex organism" metabolism and switching over to the old-fashioned fermentative "grow as much as you want and never die" metabolism, suggesting that oxygen in some form might be able to restore cancer cells to a noncancerous state. Certainly the unrestrained growth and immortality of cancer cells, as well as the presence of lactic acid in some tumours, is suggestive that there might be something here worth a much closer look.

Now let's get back to booze. Alcohol, from the point of view of the yeast organisms that produce it, is a waste product. It's "yeast pee," if you will. As you might well imagine, there's a limit to how easy it is to live in your own waste products, and for yeast, fatal squalor sets in at about 14 to 18 percent alcohol. So, if you start off with a glass of grape juice, and add some yeast, the yeast cells will grow and reproduce using the sugar in the juice for food, producing ever more alcohol until they finally die in a somewhere-around-16-percent solution of alcohol in grape juice—that's wine. Technically, you can start with any fruit juice at all, and what you get after the yeast does its thing is called wine, but it's not likely something you'd want to drink! The fact that living things don't like alcohol concentrations over about 18 percent is, of course, the origin of the antiseptic properties of alcohol, and the reason your physician swabs your skin with it before giving you a shot.

"Alcohol, from the point of view of the yeast organisms that produce it, is a waste product. It's 'yeast pee,' if you will."

Adding enough sugar to wine can sometimes restart fermentation reactions, producing carbon dioxide and leading to sparking wines and champagne. Interestingly enough, there's a lot to be learned from a glass of bubbly. The bubbles form at rough spots on the surface of the glass and can serve as "seeds" that enable the gas to come out of the solution. A similar process leads to the use of silver iodide crystals in the seeding of clouds to form raindrops, and to the creation of a device called a "bubble chamber," which reveals the tracks of charged particles via the formation of a trail of bubbles in a liquid—a device that earned its inventor a Nobel Prize.

Beer is actually a much more sophisticated and subtle beverage than wine in many ways. In this case, you start off with grains, which contain starches. Starches are long chains of sugar molecules that have to be broken down with heat and water in order to release sugar that the yeast can work with. This is what "brewing" is—turning grain and water into a sweet liquid called "wort," to which yeast is added. With the yeast happily fermenting the wort you might well ask how one keeps other organisms from getting in and spoiling things. For example, while the bacteria that make lactic acid are lovely for making sauerkraut and yogurt, you don't want them in beer! The time-tested solution to this problem is to add hops—a close relative of cannabis—as a sort of antibiotic against bacteria that could spoil the beer. Lest you think that this is a trivial matter or restricted to beer, consider this: in long-ago times, winemakers used to put lead shot into bottles of wine. The lead compounds that formed killed the bacteria that would otherwise (fermentatively) have turned the wine to vinegar (a word that literally means "sour wine"). There was also an added bonus: many lead compounds are sweet. In Roman times these compounds were produced by cooking acidic juices in lead pans and "sugar of lead" was actually used in cooking—making today's worries about the dangers of artificial sweeteners seem almost quaint!

Now, having mentioned hops, there's a nice opportunity to discuss how beer goes bad. One of the most common complaints about bad beer is that it smells "skunky."

That smell is due to "thiols"—hop-derived cousins of alcohols in which sulphur replaces the oxygen we talked about earlier. These compounds are produced by reactions driven by light, which is why you should try to keep beer in dark places and in dark bottles. Another option is to keep beer in clear bottles and just live with any thiols by masking their smell with a slice of lime!

Skunky smelling thiols can be useful. Traces of them are added to (otherwise odourless) natural gas so you can smell a gas leak. A less successful idea was "Who Me"—a foul-smelling "anti-perfume" made of thiols that was developed by the Americans for the French Resistance to use against the Germans during World War II. The goal was to humiliate the German officers by making them smell bad. The only problem? It was a bit hard to ensure it stuck only to the intended targets. A more recent application is a mixture of eight thiols called "U.S. Government Standard Bathroom Malodor" which is used to test deodorants and air fresheners. Everything is good for something!

The word "alcohol" entered the English language in the sixteenth century, via a somewhat circuitous route from the Arabic *al-kuhl*—literally, "the kohl"—a dark powder used as eyeliner. This dark powder is a compound of the elements antimony and sulphur, made by subliming a mineral called stibnite. Sublimation, by the way, occurs when a substance passes from being a solid directly to a gas without having to become a liquid first. This is not really a well-known process, but is by no means rare and can even happen to snow if the air is dry and it's not too cold—there's a good chance you've seen the phenomenon and not really given it a thought. The connection here might seem a bit tenuous, but you might want to think of the vapour form of something as its "spirit," and alcohol itself as the "spirit" of an alcoholic mixture. Indeed, in classical Arabic, the word for alcohol is *al-gawl*, or spirit—a word that led to our English word "ghoul," and connects to the idea of strong alcoholic beverages as "spirits" of the weaker drinks they come from. The idea here is that one could take some wine, for example, and since the alcohol evaporates more easily than the water, coax the "spirit" of the wine (i.e., the alcohol) to leave so that it could be purified. The process of heating wine, collecting the vapours and cooling them down is called "distillation" and is the key to producing beverages with higher alcohol contents.

The invention of distillation was of vast importance for all the sciences, and is integral for the purification of countless substances—not the least of which is petroleum, which, during refining, is heated to separate out different components according to boiling points—a process of staggering economic significance.

Repeated distillation leads to higher and higher concentrations of alcohol, but, as you might imagine, there are limits. Drinks with more than about 40 percent alcohol tend to be rather unpleasant to drink. Since alcohol and water mix, there is a natural affinity between then two, and concentrations over about 95 percent are quite difficult to maintain as they literally pull water vapour out of the air. If you drink anything too strong in alcohol it will severely damage the tissues of your throat by ripping water from them—it's something you most definitely do not want to do.

It comes as a surprise to many people that what fire can do, so can ice. Back before there was commercial refrigeration, New Englanders made a strongly alcoholic drink called "applejack" out of fermented cider. They found that on very cold winter nights, some of the water in a container of cider would freeze on the surface. This water, in order to make a nice orderly crystal, would push alcohol out of its structure as it turned to ice. Taking the ice off left a more alcoholic beverage behind. You need very cold temperatures for this to happen (alcohol makes good antifreeze, as you can also see by the fact that a bottle of vodka in the freezer never goes solid), so one can imagine the early New Englanders were glad to find at least some benefit in the coldest nights!

"It comes as a surprise to many people that what fire can do, so can ice."

You can easily see the "applejack" effect for yourself if you let a glass of fruit juice freeze in your freezer. The ice on top will be much clearer than what's below. Lest you think this is a minor curiosity, this observation forms the basis of how silicon is refined for the electronics industry.

We've been thinking about concentrations of alcohol, but before we get numerical it's interesting to look at the qualitative effects of differing alcohol concentrations in drinks and what we can learn by just looking at a drink in a glass. One of the most significant things a wine connoisseur can look for in a glass of wine is the formation of "legs" or "tears." These drip down from a ring of clear fluid high up inside the wine glass.

How they form is actually an amazingly complex phenomenon that requires not just a mixture of alcohol and water, but exposure to the open air—observations that you can easily test by noting that legs don't form in a wineglass filled with water, nor do they form inside the wine bottle before it's been opened. If you have a glass of wine in which legs are forming, you can also stop the process by covering the top of the glass. The proper scientific term for the phenomenon is the Marangoni effect, named for the Italian physicist who studied it for his doctoral dissertation in 1865. One hopes he enjoyed drinking the leftovers from his experiments!

Alcohol pulls on its own molecules somewhat less than water does, so it evaporates more easily and also spreads out on a surface more readily. Now, think of a glass of wine as a mixture of alcohol and water. Capillary action makes the mixture of both rise a little up the sides of the glass—this is just the usual slight rise of fluids near a surface they wet. As the liquid climbs up a little, the alcohol evaporates more quickly than the water. More liquid is pulled up and the process continues until a drop forms which is large and heavy enough to fall down. The process continues as long as evaporation does. Since the formation of legs needs alcohol to take place, you can use their presence as quite a good indicator of how much alcohol is in the wine. Contrary to popular belief, legs are not an indication of sweetness, as a little experimentation with wine, vodka, and sugar mixtures will show.

Distillation, of course, yields beverages with high alcohol contents and in which the Marangoni effect can be easily seen. You can see it in all the strong drinks—whiskey, cognac, grappa, vodka, and a whole list far too long to go into here. All, however, come from variants of the same basic process: ferment and distill to increase alcohol content.

Percentage of alcohol, usually by volume, is a scientific way to describe the alcohol concentration of a drink. More commonly, one speaks of "proof," where 200 proof means 100 percent alcohol, and an 80 proof vodka is 40 percent alcohol, but whence the term "proof" and why is it double the concentration?

The concept of proof goes back to the eighteenth century, when British sailors were paid, in part, with rum. Naturally, the soldiers would want to be sure that the rum had not been watered down, but without suitable laboratories and test equipment, how could they know? The idea that was hit on was to pour the rum on gunpowder and see if the gunpowder would still go off when lit. If there was too much water, the burning alcohol would not get the powder dry and hot enough to light, and one would know that the rum was of low alcohol content. The gunpowder going off was "proof" that it had not been diluted. (Just to be fair, I should note that you actually need an alcohol concentration of a little over 57 percent by volume to get gunpowder to go off, but I'm sure you get the basic idea.) If it was over 50 percent alcohol then there was 100 percent proof that it was.

This brings us back to vodka—one of the most fascinating alcoholic beverages. It even attracted the attention of Dmitri Ivanovich Mendeleyev, who created the periodic table of the elements. He made detailed studies that revealed a huge range of remarkable properties of mixtures of alcohol and water in various proportions and, based on these, concluded that vodka should be 38 percent alcohol by volume—a number rounded up to 40 percent by the authorities for simplicity and made obligatory by law. Lest you think this is a minor matter, some of my Russian friends tell me that there were times when you could legally kill the barkeep if the vodka failed to be of high enough alcohol content. Of course with 40 percent being well below 57 percent, there seems little doubt that misunderstandings associated with gunpowder tests arose, no doubt with tragic consequences.

If you still have any lingering doubts about how the consideration of alcohol can not only take you on a romp through the sciences, but also fire the passions of mankind, surely this is proof!

Another kind of proof

Most of the time, when nonphysicists ask me what I do for a living, I tell them that I'm a physicist. Physicists usually ask me what kind of physicist. This anticipates an answer of "experimentalist" or "theorist," reflecting the two main ways that physicists approach the study of nature.

The forward-backward dialogue between theory and experiment—the making of models of the world and the making of measurements of the physical world—is the foundation of science as we know it. But must a person choose to be exclusively a "theorist" or an "experimentalist"?

I can tell you first hand that one of the most remarkable experiences one can have is to actually work out theoretical/mathematical ideas and then compare them to data that one has been involved in gathering. I know of nothing else that more clearly drives home the great miracle of science than the discovery that it actually works. It really, really works. You can figure things out on paper and they correspond to reality. I continue to be awestruck by the direct experience of the fact that this is possible. I could easily imagine living in a universe so complex or random that we would just never figure anything out, and yet, wonderfully, we can.

Yes, you can do theory and experiment, and yes, you can directly see the whole connected process work, and it's wonderful … no matter who tells you differently. If you have a different theory, put it to an experimental test and see what happens.

Molecular Mixology

Frankie Solarik

Molecular mixology challenges conventional thinking about the way tastes are perceived and what is actually received on the palette.

Here is a good, basic example of what molecular mixology is all about.

The classic sidecar cocktail is traditionally prepared with brandy, Cointreau, and freshly squeezed lemon. I present this cocktail by preparing it classically and then garnishing with a top of foam, which is made of the same ingredients, along with gelatin and egg white (these provide the protein to react with and stabilize the ingredients) and nitrogen dioxide (NO_2) and carbon dioxide (CO_2).

In the end, the cocktail consists of a sparkling sidecar foam on top of a traditional sidecar, thereby presenting the same drink in two completely different textures.

Classic Sidecar

1.5 oz brandy
0.5 oz Cointreau
2 oz fresh lemon

Sidecar Foam

In a pint whipped-cream dispenser add three blanched gelatin sheets, 8.5 oz brandy, 3.4 oz Cointreau, two egg whites, and 4.5 oz fresh lemon. Add one cartridge of NO_2, and one cartridge of CO_2, and place in fridge for approximately 30 minutes to allow stabilization of gelatin. Serve on top of a classically prepared sidecar.

Alton Blakeslee and Sandra Blakeslee represent two generations in a family of four generations of science writers. Alton Blakeslee (1914–97) was a long-time science editor of the Associated Press and a regular contributor of science articles for the New York Times. His daughter, Sandra Blakeslee, has spent almost all of her career writing for the New York Times, and is the author of several books. Together, they developed these twenty tips for aspiring science writers.

Some Guidelines for Science Writing

Alton Blakeslee and Sandra Blakeslee

1. Push your enthusiasm button. If you are not interested, how can you expect to captivate your readers or listeners?

2. Think what your story really means and how best to say it. Thinking is always the hardest part. Distill your facts and purpose to the core of meaning. What is this story about? Who cares? Why are you writing it now?

3. Regard your readers not as being ignorant but more likely "innocent" of your topic and its jargon. Write for intelligent fourteen-year-olds who can follow complex material just fine but have not yet learned scientific terms or concepts.

4. Explain technical terms instantly if you must use them (and often you must), then you can use them again in that same story. But you can't use them again in your next story without defining them again. You likely won't have the exact same readers.

5. Explain the unfamiliar by comparing it with something generally familiar.

6. Put yourself on the other side of your desktop or laptop and ask yourself and then answer all the questions that might occur to you if you had never heard of the subject before.

7. Don't put all the "logs" of attribution and identification into one paragraph, just to get rid of them. Be more solicitous of your readers and sources.

8. Look for gems of detail that can make a story sparkle. Report and write with your ears as well as your eyes, seeking out phrases that say something extremely well, or colloquially, in the words of people interviewed or overheard.

9. In interviewing and researching, there is no such thing as a dumb question when you want to understand something correctly, to write about it accurately. Don't be embarrassed. Who knows everything?

10. Do not be afraid to use periods liberally. And avoid putting two unfamiliar points in the same sentence, or even the same paragraph.

11. Look for different-from-ordinary ways of expression.

12. Give your story some focus and a place to go, then quit.

13. Wring out the "water" of excess verbiage.

14. What you leave out of a story can be more important than what you leave in. Otherwise the reader may drown in non-essential detail.

15. Never let a story go without taking a second look. Is there some better or more accurate or appealing word or phrase, some lovelier expression, some sharper beginning?

16. Do not begin a story with a question, except in unusual circumstances. Instead, answer the question.

17. You likely will not get anyone to read your second paragraph unless you hook his or her interest in your first paragraph. Your opening—dramatic or soft key—counts hugely.

18. In seeking how to begin or explain something, it often helps to verbally tell a friend what your story is about. The verbal telling may help you hone your thoughts, ideas, and ways of expression.

19. Your first draft is not written in concrete. It should be intended to put all that you want to say in one place, so you can see it all better. Let that draft flow. Don't interrupt when the thinking is flowing to look up some minor detail that you can insert later. Keep it coming.

20. Digest your material. Then relax and say what you want to say.

With your story done, ask yourself:

- Is it good enough?

- Could I do better?

- Was I careless? Lazy? Tired?

- Did I really say what I wanted to say?

- Can I polish it? Find a better verb, better description, analogy?

Yes, as a writer, you probably can.

RESEARCH TOPICS GUARANTEED TO BE PICKED UP BY THE NEWS MEDIA

Chocolate! Anything that validates the public's wishful thinking that chocolate is secretly good for you is news *gold*.

A chocolate lover reacts to news that her chocolate addiction is making her smarter *and* saving the environment.

Unrealistic Sci-Fi Gadgets

Everyone is still waiting for their jet-packs, flying cars, and teleporters. Get on it, Science!

Engineers test latest invisibility cloak prototype.

JORGE CHAM © 2009

ROBOTS!! Everyone loves robots. In fact, news outlets are required by law to feature a robot story every 7 days.

Roboticist demonstrates nose-picking robot, says will soon replace humans.

Experiments That Might Blow Up The World

Nothing gets the crazies riled up like recreating conditions of the Big Bang in the only planet you have. Hope your math is right!

"Oops," say scientis-

WWW.PHDCOMICS.COM

A rt and science have encountered each other since the beginning of time, in all kinds of interesting ways—cave paintings, medical history, architecture, or Leonardo da Vinci. One of the more recent encounters— and most relevant for this volume—was in 1967, when Billy Klüver, an electrical engineer at Bell Telephone Laboratories, founded Experiments in Art and Technology (E.A.T.) with engineer Fred Waldhauer and artists Robert Rauschenberg and Robert Whitman. The artists involved in the project are now legendary in the contemporary art world but little is known of this initiative in the contemporary science communications world. Perhaps no wonder—the engineer at the helm decries any effort to force art and science into a meaningful union.

This trilogy of articles on E.A.T., starts with Billy Klüver's "Statement of Art and Science." Artists and scientists collaborating today will find it provocative. Find out more about Billy Klüver in an interview with Garnet Hertz (see page 60) from 1995. The E.A.T. project is also documented by Julie Martin, Billy Klüver's wife, who worked with him and E.A.T. since 1968.

Billy Klüver died on January 11, 2004, in his home in New Jersey. He was born in 1927 in Sweden and moved to the U.S. in 1954.

Experiments in Art and Technology

Statement of Art and Science
Billy Klüver

Art and science have developed as separate, orthogonal disciplines ever since the beginning of the human race. Science relies on a whole set of mathematical conventions which explain and prove the existence of certain phenomena. The scientist may invent new theoretical language, but only as an extension of previous knowledge, well within accepted conventions of proof and explanation. His work is always an extension of a body of universal scientific knowledge. The artist has the freedom to take his work in any direction without being loaded down with any prior theory that he has to incorporate into the work. Creative ideas in art are not bounded by the previous history of art.

To try to build a bridge, whatever that can mean, is an impossibility. I have yet to meet a scientist who takes an interest in contemporary art, or an artist whose interest in science goes beyond the "ooh and ah" stage. Artists can use in their work some version of the findings of science—for instance Rebecca Howland's interest in modelling the nuclear transport system of a cell; or James Rosenquist's use of Einstein's observation on the relative speed of objects. But I have never seen an artist who showed more than cursory interest in physical problems that concern scientists, like collisions of protons or the behaviour of electrons in electromagnetic fields. Other considerations aside, there is not enough time in one lifetime to seriously pursue both disciplines.

I myself have advocated that artists work with engineers to include engineering in their palette. But when artists make use of engineering, only practical problems are addressed, not scientific ones.

No bridge can be built between art and science if that implies fusion of certain areas of activity or thought. The gap between art and science is here to stay. Only intellectual pollution can result by misguided attempts "to bridge the gap." This is not a moral or wishful question but a factual one.

Experiments in Art and Technology (E.A.T.), 1966–2009
Julie Martin

In the 1960s, there was the growing interest among visual artists, dancers, and composers in using new technology and new technical materials generated by the rapid technological developments. Billy Klüver, a research scientist at Bell Telephone Laboratories in Murray Hill, New Jersey, began to collaborate with artists on works of art that incorporated this new technology. In 1960, Jean Tinguely presented *Homage to New York*, a machine that destroyed itself in the garden of the Museum of Modern Art; Robert Rauschenberg created the five-part environmental wireless sound sculpture *Oracle*; Jasper Johns affixed portable neon letters to his paintings *Slow Field* and *Field Painting*; Andy Warhol created his floating sculpture *Silver Clouds*; Yvonne Rainer danced to the sounds of her own breathing in *The House of My Body*; and John Cage used the movement of Merce Cunningham dancers to trigger sounds for *Variations V*.

As Klüver worked with more artists, he also realized that, despite the artists' growing desire to use new technology, the cultural separation between the artists' community and the technical community was so great that a large effort would be needed to interest engineers and scientists in working with artists.

In late 1965, Robert Rauschenberg and Billy Klüver organized a project that would provide a group of artists, dancers, and composers with the stimulating creative possibilities of the new technology and present the resulting works to a wider audience. Klüver arranged for the ten invited artists—John Cage, Lucinda Childs, Öyvind Fahlström, Alex Hay, Deborah Hay, Steve Paxton, Yvonne Rainer, Robert Rauschenberg, David Tudor, and Robert Whitman—to meet with a group of engineers from Bell Telephone Laboratories at Murray Hill, New Jersey. The artists worked for ten months in collaboration with thirty engineers and scientists from Bell Laboratories to develop technical equipment that was used as an integral part of their performances.

9 Evenings: Theatre & Engineering took place at the large space of the 69th Regiment Armory at 25th Street and Lexington Avenue in New York City from October 13 to 23, 1966. The event was widely publicized and more than ten thousand people attended the performances over the nine evenings, where each artist presented his or her work twice.

Experiments in Art and Technology (E.A.T.) was founded in 1966 by Billy Klüver, Robert Rauschenberg, Fred Waldhauer, and Robert Whitman. The decision to form the not-for-profit organization developed during the preparations for *9 Evenings: Theatre & Engineering*. It had become clear to these four that if continuing artist-engineer collaborations like the ones that had developed during their work on the *9 Evenings* were to be broadened to other artists, a major organized effort had to be made to set up the necessary physical and social conditions for such collaborations.

In November 1966, the artists and engineers who had participated in the *9 Evenings* held a meeting for artists in New York City to explore artists' interest in using the new technology. It was attended by three hundred artists, engineers, and other interested people. The reaction was positive to the idea of E.A.T. providing the artists with access to the technical world. Membership was opened to all artists and engineers, and an office set up in a loft at 9 East 16th Street in New York.

The founders of E.A.T. saw the organization acting as a catalyst to stimulate the involvement of industry and new technologies with the arts. E.A.T. worked to develop effective collaborations between artists and engineers with industrial co-operation and sponsorship.

There was an immediate response to E.A.T. from artists and the art community. However, much of the early activities of E.A.T. was focused on reaching out to the engineering community and recruiting engineers and scientists who wanted to work with artists.

Activities intended to interest and recruit engineers included visits to technical laboratories like Bell Laboratories in Murray Hill, New Jersey, or IBM Laboratories in Armonk, New York; taking a booth at the IEEE (Institute of Electrical and Electronics Engineers) convention in New York, where artists talked to engineers; weekly open houses at the E.A.T. loft at 9 East 16th Street, where artists and engineers could meet and talk informally; publication of a newsletter, *E.A.T. News*; compilation of a list of technical libraries in the New York City area open to artists. Other services to artists included loan of equipment that had been designed and built by the engineers working on the *9 Evenings*, consultation on safety of works, and approaches to industry for support of artists' projects. Equipment was lent to a performance of Carolee Schneemann's *Snows*; artist-in-residence programs were initiated at the Amalgamated Lithographers of America experimental studio and the Singer Corporation, and E.A.T. worked to secure permission for the public exhibition of an art work by Keiji Usami that employed several lasers.

A major activity of E.A.T. was the ongoing Technical Services Program, which provided artists with access to new technology for their work by matching them with engineers or scientists for a one-to-one collaboration on the artist's specific project. A part of this effort was to acquaint the technical and business communities with the needs of the artists. E.A.T. was not committed to any one technology or type of equipment like computers or holography; E.A.T. never established a laboratory or workshop, preferring for the artist to work directly with engineers in the industrial environment, which was where the technology was being made. The Technical Services were open to all artists and no judgment was made about the aesthetic value of the artist's project or idea. An effort was made to match every artist with an engineer or scientist who could help her/him. The range of artists' interests was enormous, and this diversity is reflected in the letters, proposals, and requests for technical help in the archives.

"Artists with technical requests were matched with engineers and scientists ..."

Artists with technical requests were matched with engineers and scientists for information, assistance, or longer collaborations. The system for providing information and matchings was expanded several times after 1966, including the development of the artist-engineer matching system, first using edge-notch cards to hold information on technical specialties of over two thousand engineers, as well as the initial development of a computer database of engineers and scientists for artists' reference.

In the spring of 1968, E.A.T. organized a series of lectures by engineers and scientists for artists, held at the E.A.T. loft, on technical subjects like lasers and holography; computer-generated sound and images; television; new Hexcel materials. Speakers came from academic, industrial, and government laboratories: Bell Laboratories, MIT, National Bureau of Standards, etcetera.

Another opportunity to attract engineers came about in the spring of 1968 when Pontus Hultén, director of Moderna Museet in Stockholm, asked for E.A.T.'s participation in an exhibition he was organizing, *The Machine as Seen at the End of the Mechanical Age*, to be held at the Museum of Modern Art in New York. E.A.T. announced a competition for the best contribution by an engineer to a work of art made in collaboration with an artist where the prize would be given to the engineer. The competition generated more than 140 submissions and the decision was made to show all these works at an exhibition. *Some More Beginnings*, held at the Brooklyn Museum from November 1968 to January 1969, was one of the first major international art and technology exhibitions.

Due to the early activities of the organization in attracting engineers, by 1969 there were over two thousand artist members and two thousand engineer members willing to work with artists. Expressions of interest, requests for technical assistance, and other queries came from all over the U.S. and from abroad: Europe, Japan, South America, etcetera. People were encouraged to start E.A.T. Local Groups and about fifteen to twenty were formed.

In addition to the ongoing Technical Services Program, E.A.T. began to organize and administer projects that would expand the opportunities for artists to work with different collaborators in different roles and in different parts of the world, and for artists to participate in projects whose outcome was not a formal work of art.

E.A.T. organized and administered a large-scale international collaboration to design, build, and program the Pepsi Pavilion at Expo '70, Osaka, Japan. It was initiated in October 1969 by four core artists: Robert Breer, Forrest Myers, David Tudor, and Robert Whitman. As the design of the Pavilion developed, an architect, John Pearce, several engineers and other artists like Fujiko Nakaya and Tony Martin were added to the project, and all were given responsibility to develop specific elements. All in all, twenty artists and fifty engineers and scientists contributed to the design of the Pavilion. The Pavilion opened March 1970.

The artists wanted to create a Pavilion where the visitors could explore the environment and create their own experience. The artists also conceived of the Pavilion as a performance space, and thirty-four Japanese and American artists were invited to design performances for the live programming of the space throughout the six months of Expo '70.

During the 1970s, the emergence of new hardware technologies in communications, data processing, and control and command instrumentation led to new generation of software systems, which were of great interest to the artists. E.A.T. realized that artists were not only interested in working with these systems in their own art, but also that artists could make a significant contribution to the evolution of these software systems. So E.A.T. began to generate a series of projects in which the artist participated in these areas of technological development. These interdisciplinary projects that extended the artists' activities into new areas of society included what we broadly called Projects Outside Art. They included:

The Anand Project: to develop instructional software for satellite-based education with women in a rural village in India who raise and tend milk-producing buffalo.

City Agriculture: to develop prototypes for an automated nutrient-feeding rooftop-gardening system for roofs in New York.

Children and Communication: a demonstration project with educators at NYU to link two sites with new communications equipment and invite children aged six to thirteen to interact with each other using this advanced communication technology.

Telex Q&A: a four-country telex project involving New York, Stockholm, India, and Tokyo allowing people to ask each other questions about the future.

During this period, E.A.T. also administered projects to benefit artists directly and organized artist-engineer collaborations for individual artists: among them were the cablecast of artists' videotapes over the newly opened cable television channels in New York City; and a project that allowed New York artists to travel and work for a month in India on projects of their own choosing.

Artist-engineer collaborations included a cloud sculpture set by Fujiko Nakaya for the Trisha Brown dance *Opal Loop*; a collaboration between Robert Rauschenberg, Billy Klüver, and engineer Per Biorn on a mobile, interactive set for the dance *Astral Convertible* for the Trisha Brown Dance Company, a set that could provide light and sound for the dance; and assembling a collection of ocean sounds for David Tudor's composition in the John Cage/Merce Cunningham work, *Ocean*.

"... by 1969, there were over two thousand artist members and two thousand engineer members willing to work with artists."

Current activities of E.A.T. are involved with documenting its history. The archive of E.A.T. activities from 1966–93 have been placed at the Getty Research Institute for the History of Art and the Humanities in Los Angeles, and the archive of film and other material on *9 Evenings: Theatre & Engineering* has been placed at the Daniel Langlois Foundation for Art, Science, and Technology in Montreal.

E.A.T. has initiated a project to preserve and edit more than four hundred minutes of 16mm and 35mm colour and black-and-white film footage shot in 1966 at *9 Evenings: Theatre and Engineering* to document all ten artists' performances from that event. Swedish filmmaker Barbro Schultz Lundestam will edit all ten films on video. The first film to be completed was *Kisses Sweeter Than Wine* by Öyvind Fahlström in 1996, the second was Robert Rauschenberg's *Open Score*, 1997. The films of John Cage's performance, *Variations VII*, were completed in 2008 and David Tudor's *Bandoneon! (a combine)* in 2009. The films are being released on DVD by E.A.T. in collaboration with the foundation Artpix.

In 2001, Billy Klüver produced an exhibition, *The Story of E.A.T.*—fifty panels of photos and text which hung in a single row along a wall or around a room. It occupied about seventy-five linear feet and travelled in three large suitcases. It was first shown in Rome in the summer of 2001 and has travelled to venues at museums, schools, and universities in the U.S. and Europe.

The basic idea of the artist-engineer collaboration as developed by E.A.T. has become part of the culture. Today artists do not meet with the same resistance or lack of understanding when they want to incorporate technology in their art. E.A.T. still continues to assist artists. But a measure of our success is that most artists now are able to obtain access to industry and find suitable engineering support on their own. Art schools and universities are establishing programs to encourage collaborations across disciplines, and some schools even have majors in "art and technology."

E.A.T. legitimized the artists' use of new materials and technologies, without favouring a specific technology as being more appropriate than another; and by focusing on the one-to-one collaboration between individuals we were able to do this without creating a new "ism."

Godfather of Technology and Art:
Interview with Billy Klüver

Garnet Hertz

On the cold Prairies of western Canada, in the early spring of 1994, I came across an alluring book in the library of the University of Saskatchewan: a Museum of Modern Art exhibition catalogue from 1968 titled *The Machine: As Seen At the End of the Mechanical Age*. Under its embossed metal cover was a thorough selection of machine-oriented works, from the works of Leonardo da Vinci to then-contemporary pieces, with a section organized by a group called Experiments in Art and Technology (E.A.T.) based in New York. The catalogue included a clipping of the original request for proposals for the exhibition involving artist and engineer collaborations. The address of the organization in New York was listed. Since I had already been work-ing in the field of technology and art, I decided to try to track down the group and see if they were still around.

I scribbled down E.A.T.'s address and went to a different library for the New York City telephone book and, somewhat to my surprise, found a current listing for the organization. I simply phoned it on April 19, 1995, and Billy Klüver picked up the telephone. This was our conversation.

GARNET What were some of the original ideas and goals in the formation of E.A.T.?

BILLY   The goal from the beginning was to provide new materials for artists in the form of technology. A shift happened because, from my own experience, I had worked in 1960 with Tinguely to do the machine that destroyed itself in the garden of MoMA. At that time I employed—or coerced—a lot of my co-workers at Bell Labs to work on the project. When I saw that, I realized that the engineers could help the artists; the engineers themselves could be the materials for the artists. After the event, I got besieged by a lot of artists in New York, like Andy Warhol, Robert Rauschenberg, Jasper Johns—all of them. Robert Whitman and Rauschenberg put the notion together that it should be a collaboration between artists and engineers, where they were equally represented. The idea was that a one-to-one collaboration could produce something that neither of the two could individually foresee. And that was the basis for the whole thing, and the system developed from there.

We had to do a lot of "propaganda" because in the '60s, the difference between art and engineering was an enormous canyon. We understood that we had to recruit engineers—that was the barrier we had to go through.

This whole thing spread within a year or two all over the United States. So, when an artist phoned in and said "I have this problem," we had one person on the staff that would find an engineer to help them out—and that was it.

The other thing that we did from the very beginning was organize large projects. The first one, of course, was *9 Evenings: Theatre and Engineering* in '66, out of which E.A.T. actually came. The main breakthrough in *9 Evenings* was scale. Everybody in New York was there. Practically every artist in New York helped make it a go, and about ten thousand spectators saw it. Since then we have initiated forty to fifty projects, the last one happening last summer in northern Greenland. So those are the two operations of E.A.T.: matching and making projects.

> "We had to do a lot of 'propaganda' because in the '60s, the difference between art and engineering was an enormous canyon. We understood that we had to recruit engineers—that was the barrier we had to go through."

GARNET I have a quote here … "Klüver saw many parallels between contemporary art and science, both of which were concerned basically with the investigation of life … a vision of American technological genius humanized and made wiser by the imaginative perception of artists …" Does that accurately describe your goal?

BILLY Well, it could be said better than that…. The way I see it is that artists provide non-artists—engineers or whomever—a certain number of things which non-artists do not possess. The engineer expands his vision and gets involved with problems which are not the kind of rational problems that come up in his daily routine. And the engineer becomes committed because it becomes a fascinating technological problem that nobody else would have raised.

If the engineer gets involved with the kinds of questions that an artist would raise, then the activities of the engineer go closer toward that of humanity…. Now, this is all sort of philosophical—in practice it has to do with doing it.

So, is technology a transparent medium that artists should be able to use … there's not really a moral side to technology?

Well, no. The artists have shaped technology. They have helped make technology more human. They automatically will because they're artists. That's by definition. If they do something, it automatically comes out human. There's no way you can come out and say that if art is the driving force in a technological situation, it will come out with destructive ideas. That's not possible. But what happens, of course, is that the artist widens the vision of the engineer.

GARNET And so artists can provide a conscience or humanizing element to the technology?

BILLY   Yes, that's what I mean … but that's saying it too much. There might be other "consciousnesses" that come from other sources than art. I think there is a huge consciousness inside technology that hasn't been tapped.

GARNET It seemed like the whole art and technology movement of the late '60s seemed to lose some of its initial momentum in the '70s—at least that's the impression that some texts give …

BILLY   The texts are horrible—one of the amusing things is that they tell us we've done things we never did. But the question of the momentum arose already in the first newsletter—we said that if we were successful we would disappear. We would disappear because there is really no function like E.A.T. that needs to exist in society if we were successful. It would be perfectly natural for an artist to be able to contact an engineer him- or herself. If it was natural, why should we be involved? And that's what we have stated from the beginning—and of course that is what has happened. The universities, the computer graphic societies, artist societies, and organizations like your own—it was inevitable.
   People in New York wanted us to move in, to set up labs with all of the equipment, but we constantly refused. It was not a matter of institutionalizing. I'm very pleased that the initial attitude was like that because it meant that we could still exist. To institutionalize anything in this area is dangerous and self-destructive. It's just a matter of solving problems, and you can do that forever.
   It makes sense that people critical of E.A.T. have misinterpreted it as being very institutionalized—when in reality it is quite the opposite. The main thing is that we never anticipated the growth in the late '60s—and you had to take care of it—so you needed a staff.

GARNET How do you "match" artists through E.A.T.?

BILLY   Almost anybody who calls us, we help. I never ask to see people's paintings or anything that they do. Usually the conversation starts off with "I have a problem …" After that, I always ask the same three questions when somebody calls me about something: (1) how big is it, (2) how many people are going to see it, and (3) is it inside or outside? If there is no answer to any one of these three questions, like "It could be as big as you want," or "It could be inside or outside," you know that he or she has no idea of what they're doing. They haven't taken into account the reality of the project. If you can get down to the reality of the problem, you can usually solve it in a few minutes. It's amazing how simple it is to find the answer.

While matching, I always have the artist call the engineer directly. There is a lot of intimidation there in the first place. E.A.T.'s most important role is to eliminate the initial intimidation. Once the engineer and the artist get to talk together—if there is anything there—it will happen. If there isn't, it will die in ten seconds. It's happened that way for over thirty years.

GARNET So there's no mission of E.A.T. overtaking the art scene?

BILLY Overtake? It's already been overtaken. Namely that people can talk about it without being terrified. This has been what I've said since the early '60s. Nobody then could believe that an artist could talk to an engineer …

For example, do you know the group called S.R.L.?

GARNET Yeah, Survival Research Laboratories with Mark Pauline.

BILLY We talk now and then. I see them as being brilliant—just totally brilliant. He is of the next generation and he understands the business of "getting things done." And that's what it's all about—*getting it done*—that's the key to all of it. Artists will often be intimidated by "Oh, it's a problem"—they think a power plug is an enemy.

> "Once the engineer and the artist get to talk together—if there is anything there—it will happen. If there isn't, it will die in ten seconds. It's happened that way for over thirty years."

GARNET So, what if somebody were to call you the "Godfather of Technology and Art"?

BILLY Well, I guess in a way it's probably true. However, [Vladimir] Tatlin is to me the real Godfather—the constructivist artist. That group embraced technology, and embraced it in terms of art.

Many people wanted E.A.T. to be about art and science, but I insisted it be art and technology. Art and science have really nothing to do with each other. Science is science and art is art. Technology is the material and the physicality.

However, as far as that goes—other people would have to agree with you, but I think that's probably true—that I would be the Godfather of Art and Technology.

It's one thing to write a poem about science; quite another to use a laboratory technique instead of words to author a new creative work. Christian Bök is a Canadian experimental poet who teaches at the University of Calgary. He creates original aesthetic entities by taking up, at once, concepts and media whose entanglement creates an entirely new work. For this book, Bök presents a triptych: an existing poem, a related image, and a grant proposal for a poem that is, at this moment, in process in a biology laboratory. The art and science in this poem, called "The Xenotext Experiment," cannot be disentangled: the poem is a genetically engineered text.

"The Xenotext Experiment" may appear at first glance to refute Billy Klüver's statement that art and science cannot be reconciled. However, even though there is scientific work involved in the creation of this artwork, the end goal is to create a new text. There also may be some potential for new scientific knowledge.

A Virus from Outer Space

Christian Bök

Language
is a virus
from outer space.

Language
is a pursuer
of covert aims.

Language
frames our
virus as poetic.

Language
tapers our
vicious frames.

Language
for a sum is
a corrupt sieve.

Language
for us promises
a curative.

This poem consists of a series of anagrams based upon the famous aphorism by
William S. Burroughs.

BELOW This image depicts a silkscreen of Christian Bök's poem, "A Virus from Outer Space"—a silkscreen, produced by the poet in collaboration with the printmaker Eveline Kolijn, who has created a sculpture of the protein that grants radioresistance to the bacterium *Deinococcus radiodurans*, the host for Bok's genetically engineered text (in progress).

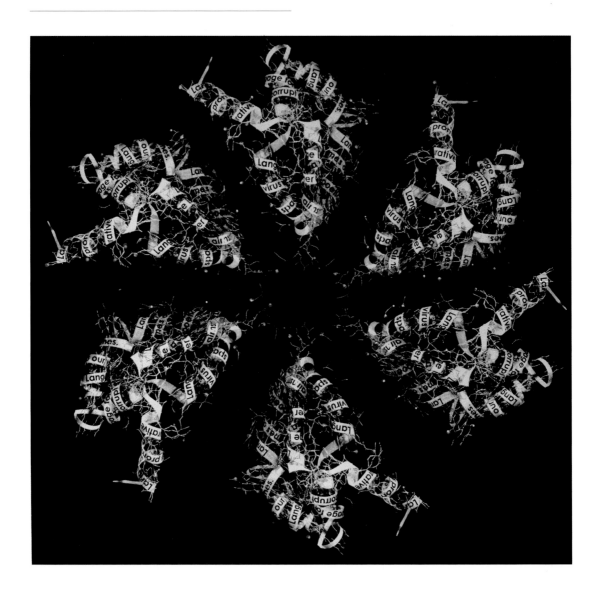

The Xenotext Experiment

Christian Bök

Introduction

"The Xenotext Experiment" is a literary exercise that explores the aesthetic potential of genetics in the modern milieu—doing so in order to make literal the renowned aphorism of William S. Burroughs, who declared that "the word is now a virus."[1] In this experiment, I propose to address some of the sociological implications of biotechnology by manufacturing a "xenotext"—a beautiful, anomalous poem, whose "alien words" might subsist, like a harmless parasite, inside the cell of another lifeform.

Thinkers as diverse as Pak Wong (a cybernetic expert), Eduardo Kac (a multimedia artist), and Paul Davies (an astronomic expert) have already begun to speculate that even now scientists might store data by encoding textual information into genetic nucleotides, thereby creating "messages" made from DNA—messages that we can then implant, like genes, inside cells, where such messages persist, undamaged and unaltered, through myriad cycles of mitosis, all the while preserved for later recovery and decoding.

Wong, for example, has enciphered the lyrics to "It's a Small World After All," storing this text as a strand of DNA inside *Deinococcus radiodurans*—a bacterium resistant to inhospitable environments. Wong argues that, in a world of fragile media with limited space for storage, DNA might permit us to preserve our cultural heritage against planetary disasters: "organisms [...] on Earth for hundreds of millions of years represent excellent candidates for protecting critical information for future generations."[2]

Kac has also used a genetic process of encipherment in his artwork called *Genesis*—a project intended to show that "biological processes are now writerly."[3] Kac encodes a short verse from the Bible into a strand of DNA, which he then inserts into a microbe, exposing the germ to doses of mutagenic radiation. Kac suggests that, by "editing" such a text through mutation, we can foster an unguided, aleatory message in a more innovative form, rather than accept the dominant, biblical passage in its last inherited form.

Davies has gone so far as to propose an extravagant speculation, suggesting that, instead of sustaining a radio beacon through many millennia or instead of projecting a large vessel across vast distances, aliens wishing to communicate with us might have already encoded messages in DNA, sending out legions of small, cheap envoys—self-maintaining, self-replicating machines that perpetuate their data over eons in the face of unknown hazards: "fortunately, such machines already exist"—and "they are called living cells."[4]

These three thinkers have all suggested the degree to which the biochemistry of living things has become a potential substrate for inscription. Not simply a "code" that governs both the development of an organism and the maintenance of its function, the genome can now become a "vector" for heretofore unimagined modes of artistic innovation and cultural expression. In the future, genetics might lend a possible, literary dimension to biology, granting every geneticist the power to become a poet in the medium of life.

Proposal

Stuart Kauffman (a MacArthur Fellow, who is now the iCORE [Informatics Circle of Research Excellence] Chair for the Institute of Biocomplexity and Informatics at the University of Calgary) has agreed to lend me the expertise of his lab during its free time so that I might compose an example of such "living poetry." I propose to encode a short verse into a sequence of DNA in order to implant it into a bacterium, after which I plan to document the progress of this experiment for publication. I also plan to make related artwork for subsequent exhibition.

I plan to compose my own text in such a way that, when translated into a gene and then integrated into the cell, the text nevertheless gets "expressed" by the organism, which, in response to this grafted, genetic sequence, begins to manufacture a viable, benign protein—a protein that, according to the original, chemical alphabet, is itself another text. I hope, in effect, to engineer a primitive bacterium so that it becomes not only a durable archive for storing a poem, but also a usable machine for writing a poem.

I foresee producing a poetic manual that showcases the text of the poem, followed by an artfully designed monograph about the experiment, including, for example, the chemical alphabet for the cipher, the genetic sequence for the poetry, the schematics for the protein, and even a photograph of the microbe, complete with other apparati, such as charts, graphs, images, and essays, all outlining our results. I also want to include (at the end of the book) a slide with a sample of the germ for scientific inspection by the public.

I do foresee enlarging charts and photos from this exercise so that I can display them in a gallery—but I also plan to create other works of conceptual art inspired by the structure of the encoded, genetic poem itself. I plan, for example, to submit the gene to DNA 11 (www.dna11.com), a company that makes giclée prints of abstract artworks produced through DNA fingerprinting, and I also hope to build a colourful sculpture of the gene itself out of dozens of Molymod Molecular Kits (www.molymod.com).

I expect that the poem is going to be concise, probably about fifty words in length (so that the encoded, genetic text can easily fit into the genome without compromising the function of the organism itself). I have yet to determine what the poem might say under the biochemical constraints of this experiment, but I do expect that the work is going to address the relationship between language and genetics, doing so self-reflexively and self-analytically. I want to convey the beauty of both the poetic text and its biotic form.

Rationale

Stuart Kauffman is a renowned theorist who has argued that the complex, but orderly, structure of every living system arises spontaneously out of underlying principles of self-organization—principles no less important than the laws of selective evolution. First trained as a specialist in the humanities (with the intention of becoming a poet), he has instead gone on to pursue a career in the study of genetics. We believe that our overlapping territories of interest make us ideally matched to undertake this project.

My own artistic activity testifies to the fact that I have always regarded my poetry as a "conceptual experiment," reminiscent of work done in think tanks, where scientists might indulge in hypothetical speculations, putting into play the propriety of reasoning itself. Just as the "pataphysics" of Alfred Jarry, for example, might intermix technical concepts with aesthetic conceits so as to create an archive of "imaginary solutions,"[5] so also does my own artwork strive to create such a hybrid fusion of science and poetics.

We hope that our unorthodox experiment might serve to integrate two mutually isolated domains of research—domains that might not have, otherwise, had any reason to interact, except under the innovative conditions of this artistic exercise. Our collaboration allows us to explore the aesthetic potential of a "literary genetics," even as the project affords us an opportunity to refine methods for the biological encryption of data—methods that might be applied to domains as varied as cryptography, epidemiology, and agrobusiness.

We foresee that, if science can perfect the process for implanting lengthy, textual information into a germ, we might not only provide a secure method for transmitting secretive documents, but we might also "watermark" cells so as to track the movement of either microbial diseases or botanical products. We believe that, with such a burgeoning technology, books of the future may no longer take on the form of codices, scrolls, or tablets, but instead they may become integrated into the very life of their readers.

Conclusion

"The Xenotext Experiment" strives to "infect" the language of genetics with the "poetic vectors" of its own discourse, doing so in order to extend poetry itself beyond the formal limits of the book. I foresee that, as poetry adapts to the millennial condition of such innovative technology, a poem might soon resemble a weird genre of science fiction, and a poet might become a breed of technician working in a linguistic laboratory. I hope that my project might, in fact, provoke debates about the future of science and poetics.

Even though this whimsical, aesthetic endeavour might accent some of the ironies in the ominous conceit of the poet Christopher Dewdney—who has argued that "language may be regarded as a psychic parasite which has genetically earmarked a section of the cortex for its own accommodation"[6]—my attempt to build a literary parasite in the form of a "word-germ" has only the most minuscule, most negligible, chance whatsoever of producing any dangerous contagion (despite the alarmism of critics outside of biology).

"I hope that my poem might urge readers to reconsider the aesthetic potential of science, causing them to recognize that, buried within the building blocks of life, there really does exist an innate beauty, if not a hidden poetry—a literal message that we might read, if only we deign to look for it."

My project merely highlights the degree to which the modern, social milieu has now taken for granted that the discursive structures of epidemiology (as seen, for example, in such notions as "viral marketing" or "viral computing") might apply to the transmission of ideas throughout our culture. If the poet plays "host" to the "germ" of the word, then the poet may have to invent a more innovative vocabulary to describe this "epidemic" called language. I feel that my project goes some way toward fulfilling this function.

I also believe, moreover, that such a poem might begin to demonstrate that, through the use of nanoscopic, biological emissaries, we might begin to transmit messages across stellar distances or even epochal intervals—so that, unlike any other cultural artifact so far produced (except perhaps for the *Pioneer* probes or the *Voyager* probes), such a poem, stored inside the genome of a bacterium, might conceivably outlast terrestrial civilization itself, persisting like a secret message in a bottle flung at random into a giant ocean.

I believe that, in the end, my own project draws concerted attention to the sublimity of language itself, teaching us about the wonders of science in a manner that might seem more engaging to a layperson untrained in biochemistry. I hope that my poem might urge readers to reconsider the aesthetic potential of science, causing them to recognize that, buried within the building blocks of life, there really does exist an innate beauty, if not a hidden poetry—a literal message that we might read, if only we deign to look for it.

1 William S. Burroughs, *The Ticket That Exploded*. (New York: Grove Press, 1967), 49.

2 Pak Chung Wong, et al., "Organic Data Memory Using the DNA Approach," *Communications of the ACM*, vol. 46.1 (January 2003): 98.

3 Eduardo Kac, "Genesis," in *Telepresence & Bio Art: Networking Humans, Rabbits, and Robots*. (Ann Arbor: University of Michigan Press, 2005), 249–63.

4 Paul Davies, "Do We Have to Spell It Out," *New Scientist* 2459 (August 7, 2004): 30–31.

5 Alfred Jarry, *Exploits and Opinions of Doctor Faustroll, Pataphysician*, Trans. (Simon Watson Taylor. Boston: Exact Change, 1996), 22.

6 Christopher Dewdney, *The Immaculate Perception* (Toronto: House of Anansi Press, 1986), 59.

Iconic images of science dominate the public imagination about what the scientific enterprise is all about—pictures of the Milky Way, models of DNA, X-rays, chaos theory, and beakers on benches. But the use of visuals—drawings, in particular—to depict or test scientific understanding is a hugely underused tool in communicating about science. We shape and are shaped by visual depictions of scientific processes, probably more than you think. So don't just tell me what you know, show me that you understand. There's a test. Rosalind Reid has been leading workshops on the power of pictures in science since 2005. She is director of the Initiative in Innovative Computing at Harvard University, and was the editor of American Scientist from 1992 to 2008.

Talking Pictures

Rosalind Reid

The man in the slightly rumpled jacket rose from the table, rolled up the large sheet of paper on which he'd been drawing, and tucked it under his arm. "Now," he said, "I can finally explain to my dean what I do!"

The occasion was an interdisciplinary meeting of scientists and engineers, and the scene was a large hotel meeting room populated with linen-draped round tables. During the previous half-hour, the scientists at each table had fiddled with markers and stared at blank sheets of flip-chart paper before beginning their workshop task: conveying bits of their life's work in simple cartoons. As they showed one another their scratchings, they had begun talking, inquiring, refining: engaging in a shared exploration of how pictures can aid understanding of science. I like to think that they all left knowing what the professor in the rumpled jacket knew: that in crafting a single effective scientific drawing, a scientist can learn something new about science and also about the essence of human communication.

In the past decade, science has entered the age of visualization. Display technologies and graphics software are now thoroughly integrated into the doing of science and are especially essential to the social aspects of science—collaboration and communication. The LCD projector, imaging and animation software, and the graphics capabilities of scientific software provide easy access to vivid colour, animation, and interactivity for interpreting the most complex ideas and aspects of data and methodology.

Some say scientists are poor users of visual tools. I disagree, but my argument here has nothing to do with the dazzling array of visualization techniques now on the market. Instead, I invite the reader to consider how the simplest forms of visual expression—the pencil sketch, the blackboard diagram—elegantly convey the essence of scientific passion and purpose, elucidating and expressing the scientific mind and mediating the iterative, dialectical development of scientific knowledge. I offer as evidence observations from my own experience, but the argument is rooted in ancient tradition. The act of sketching to communicate draws a deep connection between the ancient human art of communicating with gesture and image and a major contemporary challenge: how to talk about science across chasms of understanding.

ABOVE Lascaux horse.

The pictures and symbols in rock paintings and carvings are among the earliest surviving records of ancient stories and cosmologies. Many seem mystical and fanciful, but frequently one can discern practical or didactic elements. The famous cave paintings of Lascaux incorporate arrows or spears that appear carefully aimed for a kill shot. This is sometimes cited as the earliest surviving scientific illustration—a tool for training young paleolithic hunters in essential anatomy.

The traces left by scientists tend to take the form not of paintings or drawings but of writings. Scholars studying the history and practice of science spend much of their time analyzing these inscriptions. By focusing on the formal rhetoric of science, these studies necessarily slight informal aspects of scientists' communication. Many scientists are marvellous teachers and storytellers, modes of discourse that connect with the ancient cave painters and go a step further, engaging the communicator in discerning meaning, and building and sharing a mental model of it, in order to communicate. Scientific writing, the act of preparing a paper for journal submission, is a different sort of act.

I learned this, slowly and painfully, when I went to work for a science magazine in 1990.

Writing up one's work for publication is a core activity for a scientist; writing for audiences outside one's discipline is not. Most scientists are inexperienced with popular writing, even though they spend a considerable proportion of their working hours at the keyboard.

In the preparation of a scientific text, a scientist dons a straitjacket, largely setting aside the colourful metaphors that keep undergraduates' attention in the lecture hall to meet the requirements of the list-like and listless Materials and Methods Section and the defensively written, perhaps numbered Conclusions. A submitted scientific manuscript or proposal for funding is analogous to a lawyer's brief: a presentation of argument and evidence to a shadowy and skeptical group of referees.

"Writing up one's work for publication is a core activity for a scientist; writing for audiences outside one's discipline is not."

When invited to explain their science in an ordinary written narrative, many (though certainly not all) scientists find themselves trapped in this learned mode of discourse. During my years as an editor at Sigma Xi's *American Scientist*, I found that my attempts to help scientists write in a conversational tone about science often induced grave discomfort. For some, it was as if they had learned a special language for writing about science, and when creating text for publication could express science only in that language.

I was instructed to spend about half my time as an article editor on illustration development, a process initially puzzling to someone steeped in traditional journalism. A journalist learns and understands much as a scientist does, by asking endless questions. Yet gradually I found that most of the time, drawing pictures surpassed asking questions as the way to poke through misunderstandings and jargon and finally reach, between scientist-author and editor, a shared conception of the science we needed to communicate.

I'd always relied on writing as a way to understand, but illustration was a revelation. And through working on pictures, I came to understand just how slippery words are.

Imagine that a magazine article by a scientist-author includes this statement: "There may be an association between fossil-fuel use and climate change." Scientific prose tends to be full of causation-avoiding qualifiers: may, might, suggest, suppose, tending to, etcetera. The words say virtually nothing, but imagine that this is as strong a statement as the exceedingly circumspect author is willing to make in print. The next challenge is how to illustrate such a text. An easy solution is to forage for images. Smokestack? Polar bear? Hockey-stick graph? These are images laden with meaning in the context of current controversy, but their encodings likely have nothing to do with the scientist-author's message. It is time, I'd suggest, to sketch. Suppose the author penning those carefully qualified words is asked to sketch an illustration of the science linking fossil-fuel use to climate change. Choices must be made in reducing a system, a set of observations, or a concept to a drawing in two dimensions. What elements of the climate system do you include? What human inputs? Even that most ambiguous of glyphs, the arrow, has a strong meaning in such a sketch. In science a hand drawing or diagram is an abstraction, a toy model, just the skeleton of the argument. Choices of elements and their relations must be made explicitly, with the knowledge that a strong impression will be left in the viewer's mind.

Again and again during my time as an editor, I would send a proposed sketch to an author and find that it revealed to the scientist a flawed understanding of

BELOW Sketches of old and new concepts of the proton. The first sketch is David Schneider's original sketch, which was sent to authors. The second is Tom Dunne's sketch of the new concept after discussion with authors. Photo courtesy *American Scientist*.

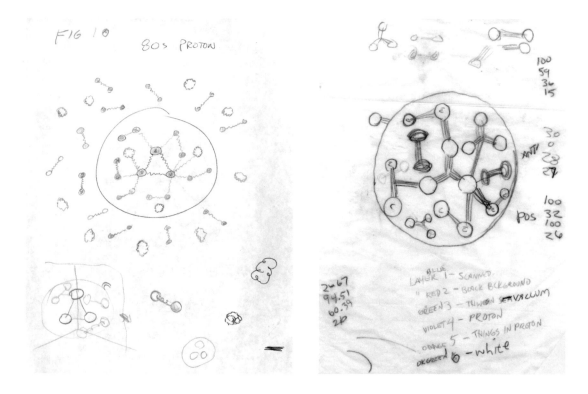

the science described in the accompanying text. No, it works like this, he would respond, sending back a markup or a new sketch. We no longer use a spring to represent the strong force that binds particles in the atomic nucleus; we use heavy rubber bands, because we now understand these connections as flux tubes. I see, I would say—and then I'd revise the text.

Community life at the Kavli Institute of Theoretical Physics (KITP) of the University of California at Santa Barbara centres on the traditional physics talk and conversation at the blackboard. Although graduate students, post-docs, and faculty can be found facing the computer screens on their desks for hours at a time, KITP provides sufficient blackboard real estate to rival the square footage of those display screens. Hallways, meeting rooms, even a courtyard have been designed around blackboards.

When I visited KITP as journalist-in-residence in 2003, I was privileged to experience talks by some of the most famous physics communicators of our day. PowerPoint slide presentations were widespread by that time, but there was ample opportunity to savour the craft of the blackboard talk.

What is the blackboard talk? In theoretical physics, at least, a good chalk talk advances an idea through the interplay of diagrams and mathematical reasoning, sketched sparely so that the listener's mind will hold and follow the thread. Words are spoken, not typed onto bulleted lists on slides; diagrams and the equations that describe them are laid out and refined together.

Consider the recent talk by Joe Polchinski of KITP shown in the snapshots here (from a KITP podcast). Joe opens his talk with casual drawings to show just what aspects of strings and superstrings he will discuss, then moves from left to right to frame details of his proposition in blackboard panels. As questions are raised and earlier arguments refined, he moves back and forth to replace or elaborate on earlier sketches. When the sketching is finished, the storyline is

ABOVE Joe Polchinski, drawing and teaching.

complete—and, importantly, viewable all at once. Yet the sketch is skeletal, leaving open questions everywhere, inviting debate and elaboration.

I found myself thinking about chalk talks recently while reading about the recently discovered Archimedes Palimpsest, which provides fresh evidence of the importance of drawing. Analyzing the diagrams found in the revealed codex, scholar Reviel Netz of Stanford emphasizes that some are intentionally imprecise. As Archimedes developed his mathematics for science, Netz writes in *The Archimedes*

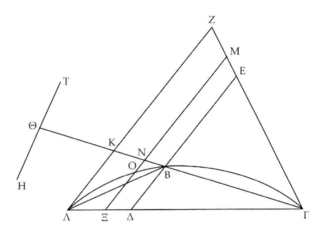

The Palimpsest diagram

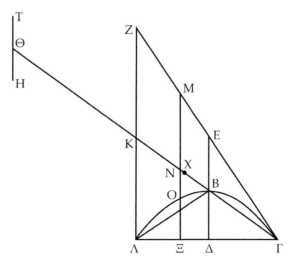

RIGHT Archimedes sketches. These are sketches by William Noel that were used to develop Figure 4.10 of *The Archimedes Codex* by Reviel Netz and William Noel. One is Archimedes' imprecise diagram in the palimpsest; the other is the strictly correct way of drawing the diagram, for comparison.

A modern illustration

Codex, he drew on the "deeply austere, deeply non-pictorial" drawing tradition of the Greek geometers. The diagrams carefully avoided realistic representation of objects under discussion, so as not to illustrate any particular case. Archimedes and his colleagues used drawings to force the reader's mind to generalize, to participate in a thought experiment broader than the case at hand. It is humbling to compare many modern scientific illustrations, with their 3-D icons, drop shadows, and rainbow hues, with Archimedes' spare and elegant lines and curves. And it is not surprising that theoretical physics would be a place where non-pictorial diagrams remain a crucial tool of modern scientific thought.

In the written record of physics, Richard Feynman's diagrams spring to life instantaneously in 1949, scattered through the text of an article offering a new theory. It is some time before they propagate and mutate in the way physical theories themselves do, in a clamour of argument and the intense interactions between young physicists and their mentors.

Most people who have experienced a blackboard lecture on quantum interactions in physics in recent decades have seen the space time diagrams that Feynman invented: electron meets positron, and off comes a photon. They may look to the untrained eye like storytelling devices, but these doodles are special. Their origin and meaning in physics has to do with a particular mode of thought; they serve as a calculational and bookkeeping tool for mediating a deeply mathematical discourse.

In my first attempts at writing about particle physics, I found Feynman diagrams to be a great help. I wasn't a Feynman follower, but I'd seen enough of the lectures to appreciate his gifts as a communicator. I formed this naive hypothesis: Feynman came up with the diagrams as a way to communicate with himself, to jot down an idea on a napkin so that he could carry it off in his pocket and work on it later. Here, I thought, might be a superb example of a fellow who represented the continuum, from visual thinking through visual collaboration to visual teaching and communication.

The "visual thinking" part of this hypothesis did not hold up well.

During my 2003 stay in California, I asked to spend an afternoon with photocopies of uncatalogued Feynman material in the Caltech Archives. Feynman indeed wrote on napkins, hotel stationery, anything at hand. I spent a pleasant afternoon rummaging through the boxes of equations and notes. But I found scant evidence in these papers that Feynman had doodled while developing the ideas that he expressed with the diagrams in 1948 and 1949.

I understood the story of the diagrams better after I read *Drawing Theories Apart*, by David Kaiser of MIT. Physicists who worked with Feynman recall that he indeed used the diagrams to work out his revolutionary ideas in quantum electrodynamics—on the blackboard, often with young colleagues. The early diagrams didn't work well as devices for communicating his ideas; when he first presented them, at a conference in the Pocono Mountains in 1948, Kaiser has said that Feynman's colleagues took the chalk from his hand. It was his young colleague Freeman Dyson who created from them a useful language for physics after colleagues dismissed Feynman's early doodles as non-rigorous.

This is a cautionary tale on several levels. The diagrams made intuitive sense to Feynman, but they may have been too rooted in his own intuition; others needed to see the derivation of his hypotheses or work through the underlying equations to discern meaning in the new language he was proposing. In other words, a community process was required to make the implicit knowledge in his diagrams explicit. As with any language, scientific drawings gain meaning through successful use in a social context.

Once Feynman's new diagrammatic shorthand took hold, it turned out to have enormous power. Feynman diagrams have been modified by each generation of physicists to do important work, both in the working out of problems and the sharing of ideas and solutions. Just as the solution found by the man in the rumpled jacket came about through conversation with his tablemates, trying out and iterating combinations of spoken word and sketch, so did Feynman's diagrams find their usefulness through a social process.

The drawing workshops began after a Sigma Xi chapter invited me to talk about how illustrations were developed for *American Scientist*. Before the invitation, I had not considered carefully what went on in the highly iterative and conversational process of developing didactic and conceptual illustrations and data displays, even though this was half of my work as an editor.

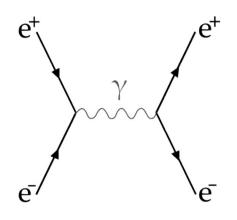

ABOVE A basic Richard Feynman diagram.

Creating the talk was such fun that I conceived an experiment: after giving a short version of the picture talk, I asked mixed groups of scientists to sketch aspects of their science and talk about the sketches among themselves and with the magazine's art and editorial staff. The initial notion was simply to act out the illustration development process and find out what we could learn from doing that together. The exercise turned out to be a nice meeting icebreaker, and so the workshops continued. Soon we observed that students who had engaged in research were especially adept at explaining their work in drawings, and so began intergenerational workshops.

The character of the workshops changed with their settings and participants. A group of aquatic and environmental biologists preferred to sketch co-operatively rather than individually. At a Mexican university, participants wanted to critique each other and play a game guessing the meaning of one another's drawings. These experiences refined my understanding of the act of sketching to communicate. It is a process deeply influenced, as communication itself is, by culture and by feedback from peers and audience.

In 2005, I began working with Felice Frankel of MIT and others to launch a new set of workshops focused on the role of images in conveying meaning in science. In an initial experiment during a conference, scientists came together with designers and professional communicators in a space equipped with drawing tools and objects for building tangible models. This social sketching became the basis of the Image and Meaning Workshops (a continuation of the Image and Meaning project Felice had launched with a 2001 conference) and then, later, an aspect of Felice's Picturing to Learn student workshops.

The lessons of Image and Meaning and Picturing to Learn are important to understanding the visual communication of science. First, all participants find that making a good drawing to communicate a scientific concept or result is difficult, for surprising reasons. In stripping a problem down to its bones, a drawing reveals the structure underlying scientific thinking. If one's understanding is incomplete or a certain visual metaphor is ill-fitting, others will derive an incorrect understanding as they parse the drawing. In each of these workshops, drawings emerge through hours of iteration. Rarely has the product of this iteration been a "successful" representation; rather, we have found that a deep understanding of the underlying science has spread among the group. Through drawing, they have come to understand.

"In stripping a problem down to its bones, a drawing reveals the structure underlying scientific thinking."

Collaborative drawing workshops are resource-intensive and, frankly, exhausting. Happily, Picturing to Learn has also confirmed that there is important challenge and reward in merely attempting to draw on one's own for the purpose of communicating science. At the core of this project has been a series of exercises in which college-level science students produce a sketch of a concept they have been taught. They are instructed to produce a drawing to communicate the concept to a high-school student, and then to identify the elements of their drawings that accomplish the communication.

The thousands of drawings produced by these participants have been of widely varying style, content, and quality, but most share an important property: they display to the instructor, in ways that conventional tests do not, misperceptions of the subject matter that persist after the students' exposure to lectures, labs, and readings. Like the illustration sketches sent back to our scientist-authors at the magazine, they are like X-rays revealing the bones from which these students' scientific knowledge is being built. In many cases the hip bone is not connected to the thigh bone.

The visual cortex dominates the human brain, making up one third of its outer surface. This complex and wonderfully plastic brain region has been adapted for understanding the world and perceiving patterns in it. If doing science is pattern recognition—and much of it is—then becoming a scientist can be seen partly as a matter of training the visual cortex. Hypotheses and scientific constructs are mental models, analogous to maps that we hold in visual memory. In many fields of current science, computational scientists harness computer cycles to process huge quantities of data from instruments and compare the models to nature at a vast range of scales. By providing graphical representations of model parameters and outputs, the computer works with the human visual system to make sense of the workings of massively complicated systems such as genomes, airfoils, tumours, and hurricanes.

This is not work that can be done at a blackboard. So what is the place of the humble sketch in this new world? It may be more central than ever. In "Drawing Things Together," Bruno Latour wrote of the economy of drawing on paper and the power of inscription in science. A drawing creates a scale and a relation between objects. A complex natural system, process, or set of relations is stripped of less-important elements in a scientist's sketch and flattened into something that has a logic constructed from generations of drawings before it—drawings that themselves reduced and encapsulated the thinking of the scientists who drew them. There are x and y coordinates, perhaps a left-to-right flow of time. Latour refers to "drawing things together"—to the way that elements such as scale and organization are pulled together in a drawing. (Kaiser's book title plays on this concept by emphasizing how Feynman's diagrams differentiated physical theories.)

Visualization experts use the term "transfer function" to describe the algorithm that translates a data signal into attributes of the pixels in a display—hue, intensity, shading, opacity. The encodings used in data visualization are often drawn from the late-twentieth-century conventions of scientific colour graphics on paper: red for hot, blue for cold, green for biological productivity.

Today scientists and science communicators can install on their desktops the sort of software used to create hyperrealistic video games or Hollywood's new 3-D animations. It's natural to consider the power that the entertainment industry's new "language" might hold for addressing science's visualization challenges. But I hope that the parsimonious inclinations of scientists hold sway in the new video-enhanced world. A rich visual shorthand has already been developed through the sketching tradition: a squiggly arrow for electromagnetic radiation, a gap and angled line segment denoting a break in a circuit or feedback loop. Biology's conventions, arising from a naturalistic tradition of drawing from life, are more curvilinear and rich in icons yet still wonderfully simple, as in the use of a lock and key to represent the binding of receptor molecules in biology. Each field has crafted a spare visual language, sometimes making happy and humorous connections with the drawings each of us do in childhood.

I recall the time a graduate student in a workshop sketched the "dead goat concept." To explain her study of a disease that killed goats, she populated her sketch with an assortment of stick-figure goats standing up and other goats turned upside down, x's drawn in place of their eyes. As Latour might say, she had done a wonderful job of drawing her work together: one could see on her grid how the occurrence of upside-down, x-eyed goats seemed to support a genetic hypothesis and suggest an experimental design. (She told me that the goats really did die with their legs stiffly outstretched.)

My current work has immersed me in the world of computer-enabled scientific visualization. We are learning the importance of powerful visual interfaces to help the mind's eye see new, more complex patterns in massive data sets. Yet to communicate and seek deeper understanding of science on the frontier, the best tools remain those wielded by Archimedes and his descendants—the man with the rumpled jacket, the theoretical physicist, and the student with the upside-down goats.

ABOVE A photo taken by the author at the drawing workshop at the Universidad Nacional Autónoma de México on October 14, 2004.

Sometimes, wonderful works of art are inspired by science, even though they are in no way trying to communicate anything about science, as in the case of this composition by Kelly-Marie Murphy. She is an award-winning Canadian composer whose extraordinary work has been performed and broadcast around the world. She is married to a physicist, and reveals here a scientific inspiration and a sample of the resulting work.

Dark Energy: A Composition Inspired By Science

Kelly-Marie Murphy

I view composition as a form of communication: a way of drawing connections. These connections can be between real, tangible things, or they can be interpretations of art or poetry, or anything else that catches my imagination. Regardless, they are my connections to the world outside music, but expressed in an abstract language. It is impossible to be concrete when working with sound, but I do have the advantage of being able to evoke true feelings in the listener through my choices in writing a piece.

I understand that music cannot really express anything but itself, and if I didn't give a title and a program note, the audience would make certain connections to the music of their own accord—it's what we do as human beings in order to understand something new. We reinterpret the new through our own previous experiences.

Then why bother interpreting, or naming, or imposing a connection of any kind? Because I need that as a composer. I need to be a part of the fabric that is woven between music, art, language, science, politics … It is how I communicate, and how I understand, and how I belong to the world around me.

Like many creative people, I am always on the lookout for new and interesting things outside of music that might inspire the next piece. For that reason I tend to read a great deal. In the past, I looked at many different art exhibitions. When I started working on the string quartet called "Dark Energy," I had very general ideas about dark and light, and about space, and about the coalescence of elements.

As I worked a little further with my general ideas, my husband forwarded to me a *New York Times* article that discussed the concepts of our expanding universe, and Einstein's postulate that our universe won't collapse because of a force known as "dark energy." Even though my piece isn't meant to be programmatic, I was very inspired by this idea, so I took it as a title. I like the fact that we can understand these words musically as well. Energy is as much as part of music as it is physics, and darkness can be understood as a type of musical language and quality of sound. In the end, what you hear is a musical interpretation of space: a bubbling, kinetic mixture of matter and energy that propagates forward through the musical continuum of pitch and time.

I certainly can't pretend to fully understand the science of dark energy or Einstein's postulate. I can say that I was inspired to connect that hypothetical world to the sound world I was in the process of creating. I think that audiences pick up on whatever thread I offer them and they, in good faith, attempt to make a connection between themselves, the music, and the science. What more could I ask? I have written many pieces that connect to the science world and I hope that when audiences hear pieces like "Four Degrees of Freedom," "Star Burning Blue," or "Dark Energy," they are interested in learning more about the science behind the inspiration. I'm sure that I will return to the world of science for inspiration.

My husband, Dr. Gregory Van Bavel, holds a Ph.D. in upper atmospheric physics from the University of Maryland, and is currently working in the field of operations research. In attempting to understand his world, I have attended graduate physics colloquia and read articles that I would never have encountered on my own. Although I will never understand science the way a scientist does, I will continue to make those connections and develop both sides of my brain when I attempt to create music that communicates.

FH 3349

OPPOSITE AND LEFT
Excerpt from "Dark Energy,"
published by Friedrich
Hofmeister Musikverlag. The
opening bars interpret space
as a shimmering, austere, and
isolated place.

R oger Malina is an astrophysicist at Le Laboratoire d'Astrophysique de Marseille CNRS in France and executive editor of the Leonardo publications by MIT Press, including the Leonardo Book Series and Journals. Malina is a thought leader in the art and technology world and is advocating in this article for a kind of citizen science called "micro-science." In this science, artists are involved in generating knowledge of their personal worlds by using data-collecting instruments and expressing the data aesthetically, rather than scientifically. The resulting artworks have an intimate relationship with science, and reveal something personal, peculiar, and cultural through data. It's a thought-provoking way of bringing science into a public cultural realm. Though it may not be entirely accessible to a broad public, micro-science requires an understanding or appreciation of the art world and a willingness to accept the tools of science for use in everyday life.

Making Science Intimate

Roger Malina

Many people use the cellphone for daily survival, but could not explain the difference between a photon and an electron.

One of the reasons for this is that most science does not make common sense. The vast majority of the information about the world I study as a scientist is mediated to my senses through scientific instruments; almost none is captured directly by my naked senses. I develop new words to describe phenomena I encounter that have no counterparts in daily life. I can manipulate concepts that are not grounded in my experience as a child. I can tell when my instrument is hallucinating. But this intimacy with the world mediated through instruments is not the daily experience of most people.

Micro-Science

A second reason for this disconnect of modern science and public understanding is that science is carried out mostly in guarded (mostly male) monasteries. This institutional isolation of science is a historical accident of its development, particularly because of its close connection to government and industry in wartime. But there are signs that kinds of "micro-science" are developing, a new form of people's science that is made possible by the Internet and the new public access to scientific data and instruments. Micro-science is knowledge about one's own personal world that is mediated through instruments, and that enters the personal sphere of knowledge. Science-producing communities have ownership over the knowledge they help generate, and this knowledge is locally rooted and meaningful. To coin a phrase, micro-science is to the National Science Foundation what micro-credit is to the World Bank. In other words, it puts scientific processes into the hands of individual cultural entrepreneurs, and not just the large research institutions that normally trade in this currency. I am not calling for a renewal of amateur science, but rather for embedding mediated contact with the world in everyday life. The work of technological artists is part of this movement.

One of the interesting new developments is a generation of artists that is now collecting data about their world using scientific instruments but for their cultural purposes. Not only are they making powerful art, they are making science intimate, sensual, intuitive.

Hard Humanities: The Engineering of Rapid Cultural Change

The encouragement of intimate science by artists and micro-science at all levels of society are important components of the hard humanities. The hard humanities are the disciplines in the arts and humanities that will be essential to navigating the cultural transformation we face within the next two generations. Controlling climate change, abandoning our dependency on oil for energy, creating the conditions for sustainable development—these will require as deep a cultural transformation as our ancestors accomplished over tens of thousands of years in moving from agrarian to urban societies. The work of artists in promoting art-science and art-technology collaboration is in a very real sense part of the tool kit for survival. This is a strong claim: artists using new media and new technologies are not creating playthings for rich people but are part of the rapid cultural engineering we need to do to face the burning issues of our times.

Landscape Artists

We know what a landscape artist is, and indeed landscape artists over several hundred years have helped shape our cultural imaginaries of the relationship between humans and nature. Landscape artists "appropriate" parts of the world outside the very local, in essence building "cognitive" vocabularies and grammars. A key transformation brought about by Renaissance artists and scientists was the recontextualizing of humans within the natural world, as well as the relationships of individuals to their societies. The "New Worlds" of the Americas became part of the European cultural imagination through the work of artists that accompanied the explorers and traders. When Paul Cezanne painted and repainted the scenery of Provence, he developed a visual vocabulary and artistic stance that has influenced artmaking for a hundred years. When Claude Monet or Vincent Van Gogh laid the groundwork for new ways of representing the world, it was not at all obvious at the time what the impact of this new way of seeing would be; thousands of landscape artists work today in their traditions.

Making Science Sensible

Today we can think of "climate artists" who might invoke the same degree of cultural shift. But what is a "climate artist"? A hundred years from now we will identify the climate artists working today who helped shape a new cultural imaginary. "Climate art" will somehow involve making information about our changing world perceptible and sensual—sense data accessible through instruments and not via the naked body.

Today, artists are creating for viewers intimate experiences with data about our world. As the data collectors, the artists make sensory connections to the data environment; the artist claims as his or her territory the "landscape" accessible only through scientific and technical instruments.

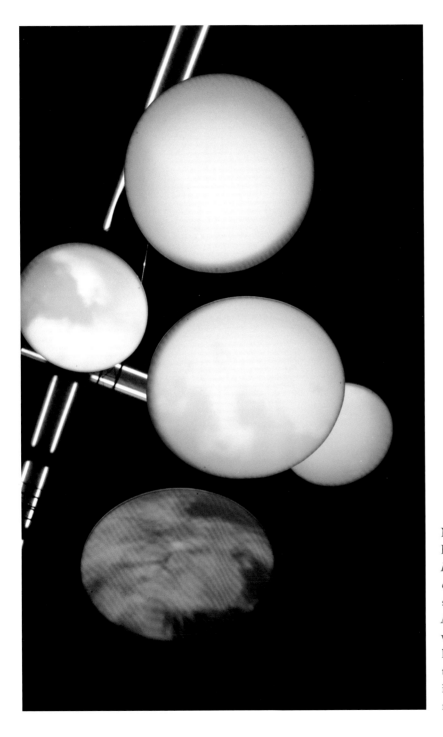

New Zealand artist Janine Randerson, in her work *Remote Senses*, takes data collected from orbiting satellites—Chinese and American—to project visualizations of metero-logical data, converting the global large-scale information to local meaning.

Beatriz da Costa with her *Pigeonblog* engages pigeon-racing communities in collecting environmental data for art purposes; the data about pollution levels is collected and made "sensible" not only as abstract data but also embedded within a particular social community.

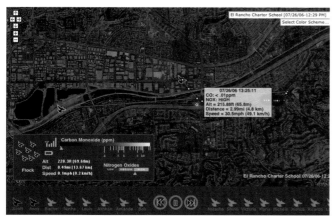

Sabine Raff monitors carbon dioxide levels and translates them through an art-making robot that draws on the walls of the gallery. Her artmaking instrument takes data about the world and converts it into "visualizations" that are the equivalent of the process used by landscape artists, but using a "mediated" sense data.

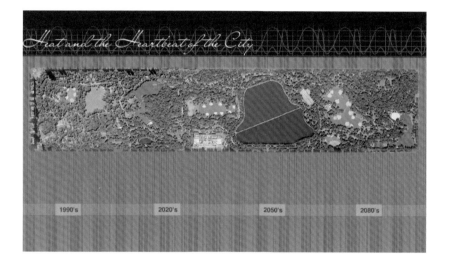

Andrea Polli works in urban environments making visible local microclimates. In her work *Heat and the Heartbeat of the City*, she sonifies small changes in ambient temperature and projects future climate change.

Argentinian artist Andrea Juan makes expeditions to Antarctica to make performances linked to the measurement of methane levels and ice melt, just as the artists on Darwin's journeys sought to make sense of the scientific data collecting.

We do not know yet what kind of artmaking will best help us transform our cultural relationship to climate, but I believe it will involve artists taking scientific data with instruments but for artistic purposes.

Katherine Moriwaki, with her "Inside/Outside" handbag, and other artists working with smart textiles create clothing and objects that respond to ambient environmental data. If we were as sensitive to methane and carbon dioxide as we are to heat and light, we could not ignore the changes in our air.

Artists and Data

The Leonardo organization and network was founded over forty years ago, when the term "computer artist" was still disputed. These artists have appropriated the computer as a means of cultural production; computers are now more widely used for cultural and social purposes than for industrial or scientific purposes. Today we see artists, involved with science and technology, working in a variety of ways on the burning issues of our times. To do this they must now appropriate the sense-data obtained using technological instruments. As I have articulated above, I think this work is part of the tool kit needed for the rapid cultural engineering ahead.

Over recent months a number of us have been developing the concept of "open observatories" that disseminate tools, techniques, data, and knowledge for carrying out projects in micro-science, intimate science, people's science and crowd sourcing. These open observatories would allow small communities to develop locally generated knowledge which can in turn be used as the basis for local action. This local action could help these communities evolve rapidly and respond to the changes that will be needed to confront climate change, break oil dependency, and master sustainable development. Open observatories would include the work of artists collecting data for cultural and artistic purposes, as well as provide a workspace for community leaders and researchers seeking to find ways to mediate personally meaningful access to scientific knowledge. Finally, open observatories might become the locus for societal retroaction on the direction and content of future science, and help establish a new social contract between science and society. Just as the open-software movement has enabled new forms of political action, so we can imagine that open-observatory approaches could over the coming decades shift science-making into a more networked and distributed form of intimate science. Open observatories might provide test beds for climate artists and other artists engaged in the hard humanities and the burning issues of our times.

The San Francisco Exploratorium is a classic in the science-centre world, a raw beauty, unselfconscious, kind of gutsy, kind of humble. You only find this mix of qualities in true originals, if you ask me. The Exploratorium grew up in the '60s in San Francisco, and after forty years in its original home, it will be moving. Part of its allure seems to be tied to the space, so the move opens up questions about the design and aesthetics of the experience with science. In an interview for this book, Susan Schwartzenberg and Shawn Lani talk about science engagement and design. They are both senior artists and long-term staff members at the Exploratorium and curators of two new exhibit environments planned for the new space. Appended to this interview is an article about the vision and design principles set by the Exploratorium's founder, Frank Oppenheimer. Prepared twenty-five years ago by long-time science writer Pat Murphy, the article outlines principles that can be considered in relation to any science communications project, and still hold today.

The Heart of the "Anti-Aesthetic" at the Exploratorium

Interview with Susan Schwartzenberg and Shawn Lani

EDITOR   So what's the status of your move?

SUSAN   We have been at our current location for forty years and have literally outgrown it. Our programs and functions just don't fit in one building anymore. The Palace of Fine Arts is an historic building and grounds. We couldn't really enlarge or easily renovate our current location into a campus with both indoor and outdoor exhibit areas, so we've been searching for another building for almost ten years. We finally found a space on the Embarcadero at piers 15 and 17. We'll have more interior space as well as a set of outdoor plazas on the waterfront. The new location is also more accessible by public transportation. Anyone who might be walking along the Embarcadero promenade can easily wander in.

SHAWN   The new location offers opportunities that we just couldn't get here. We'll be on the water with the piers reaching out into the bay, so we'll be probing, exploring, and experimenting with new programs that take advantage of our bay access and vista views.

EDITOR   That's interesting that you connect the programming to the space. I got the impression that when the museum opened so many years ago, the bunker-like space influenced the nature of the exhibits inside.

SUSAN   Yes, it was an experiment when it started. Being in a black-box laboratory space in San Francisco in 1969, you could do whatever you wanted. Frank assembled a machine shop and an eager staff to explore ways to develop exhibits and programs concentrating on perception and basic physics. Now we've "grown up" and have explored other kinds of things—like navigation, memory, mind and brain, geometry, and the biology of living systems. We also have a large teaching staff, and work with experimental media, and develop projects and exhibits for the Web. We certainly have a lot more experience. We want to take the tools and ideas that we have learned and move in newer directions, including developing new exhibits and programs on the environment and ecology, exploring the urban/natural context of our new site.

SHAWN It's like any project. At the start, you're sensitive; you're not sure where you're going. In many ways we've matured, so we're looking to broaden our scope and directly engage the city and surrounding environments.

EDITOR Let's first talk a little bit about the old space. How did the space affect exhibit design?

SHAWN When I first came to work here fifteen years ago, one of the exhibit artists, Ned Kahn, said there were a lot of restrictions working here. I thought, "What are you talking about? This place is wide open. It's one massive windowless warehouse!" Now I realize there are hidden constraints that I hadn't understood. When you first walk into the Exploratorium, there doesn't appear to be any design criteria. The exhibits are all over the place. Some works are covered in black laminate; some things are made out of old kitchen tables. Some objects are clearly artworks while others look to be found objects. What I finally came to realize was that, really, the only cardinal design rule was to have a deep respect for the learner.

EDITOR Did the industrial setting contribute to the apparent absence of design criteria, which Susan once described as an "anti-aesthetic"?

"I realized that most of the exhibits there were designed by, or supported by, corporations, and they were built by advertising agencies or contract designers and they had an ultimate social or ideological destination."

SUSAN I have been wondering why in the world I used that term! I think I wanted to get aesthetics into the discussion. There is an aesthetic here so I need to qualify the term "anti-aesthetic" a bit.

When I started working here through the mid to late '70s, I had just gotten out of art school in Chicago and my only knowledge of science museums was the Museum of Science and Industry in Chicago. After I had worked here for a while I went back for a visit. I realized that most of the exhibits there were designed by, or supported by, corporations, and they were built by advertising agencies or contract designers and they had an ultimate social or ideological destination. There was an exhibit called, I believe, "Better Living Through Chemistry" and it was produced and paid for by DuPont. The museum had lots of really great exhibits and periodic tables and everything, but the point of it was to provide entertaining science literature, ultimately aimed at recruiting workers into the field of chemistry, which was really exploding at that time. So things like that had a specific social message. In Europe it seemed to me the museums were a little bit more nationalistic. They were

OPPOSITE Exploratorium general floor shot, taken near the entrance of the museum, vertical orientation. Photo by Amy Snyder © Exploratorium promoting national products, especially the Deutsches Museum, which seemed to show all of the engines that were made by BMW and how they had participated in building airplane engines during World War II.

These museums made me realize how different the Exploratorium was. Everything was made by people on staff. None of them were trained in design, some of them may have been carpenters or engineers, artists or teachers, so they had a sense of how to make things. There were also high-school students working here who were hobbyists in their father's garage. There has always been a debate about how things look, but the early "aesthetic" that evolved was to use what was common to them and interesting to them, or simply what they found. It wasn't highly fashioned or honed, and this became sort of the aesthetic philosophy here. So it's an "anti-aesthetic" in a sense that most people wouldn't see it as being intentionally made to look a certain way. Now we wonder if in fact that unintentional look has become our look.

EDITOR It is indeed somewhat different than what you see in a lot of science centres around the world in terms of polish.

"We have a very strong design aesthetic. We just don't have an *apparent* design aesthetic."

SHAWN   It puts some people off. They may have heard of this museum, and come from a long way away and when they arrive and look around they think, "Oh my god, look at this stuff, this is made out of two-by-fours and part of an old lathe that somebody found." Other people think it's wonderful. The exhibits may appear casual, but nothing is unconsidered. If we see something that's over-designed or built for the wrong reasons, it doesn't make the floor. We have a very strong design aesthetic. We just don't have an *apparent* design aesthetic. That's the reason the museum continues to look the way that it does.

EDITOR   What shapes the aesthetic?

SUSAN   Before Frank Oppenheimer opened the museum, he built science exhibits for high-school programs that he taught in Colorado. So he wanted the exhibits to support various chapters in the physics books—concepts that helped engage students in understanding basic phenomenological questions. A lot of our early exhibits were supporting what science teachers needed in their classrooms.

When we had built up a good collection of exhibits, we also wanted other museums or teachers to be able to use our exhibits, so we designed a series of books called the "Cookbooks," which gave you the instructions for how to build the exhibits on your own. However, most people, especially in other countries, couldn't build them because they didn't have a machine shop, so we rethought the "Cookbooks" and made the "Snackbooks." These recipes helped you create exhibits using ordinary stuff found around the home. So if you didn't have a battery you could use a potato or something. This helped teachers build tabletop versions of the exhibits for their students. So, in a way, our exhibit aesthetic comes out of this idea that our science experiments are ones you could do in the classroom. The museum does struggle between trying to be a little bit more designed and being exportable to classrooms.

SHAWN   The exhibits here are just the tip of the iceberg. The material things you see and experience are the product of a holistic culture—the entire staff is involved in constant conversation and the exhibits are results of those conversations. What you find in this place is almost a throb. If you sell some of these exhibits to other museums, they just have 10 percent of what we have on the floor, and so they might not have that same kind of energy. We've actually gone a long way in creating more than just a buyer-seller relationship; we've developed partnerships that include exchanges and training, so there's culture that goes along with the exhibits.

EDITOR   That explains the juxtaposition of being an influential museum yet still looking different than the places that you've influenced.

SUSAN   We have a whole wing of the museum that redesigns our exhibits with a much different packaging for other museums—the ones we sell look really different than the ones we have on the floor.

SHAWN   Yes, there's a big difference. The exhibits we sell are highly engineered and the reason for that I think is simple: when you pay $15,000 to $25,000 for an exhibit, you don't want two-by-fours rolling through the door. The kind of whimsical quality that works here doesn't work in brand new buildings.

EDITOR   It also speaks volumes about the relationship between the exhibits and the space. As you move into the new space, how is that affecting the way you are thinking about exhibit design?

SUSAN   We are getting considerably more space at the new site. Shawn is going to be a curator for the outdoor areas of the new museum. For those areas, two thirds will feature new exhibits that have to be designed to a different criteria, for example, to hold up in fog, or dramatic temperature changes throughout the day. There's a more rigorous attention to materials and a new way of thinking about what exhibits are in an outdoor environment. They are much more connected to local phenomena and to understanding the environment. These will have a different and new aesthetic.

SHAWN   They look totally different from what you might find on the museum floor. They're kind of beautiful devices, scientific instruments that might have been set up to gather data and then the researchers walked away. We are driven as much by the emotional impact at times as the educational impact—the way that something feels in a setting or the way that something strikes you is vitally important to the overall experience.

EDITOR   Give me an example of a design decision in the new space that you had to make that you might have done differently than in the old building?

SHAWN   We are working right now on a set of outdoor exhibits for Fort Mason, which is set on national-park land. Many of the design decisions were based on how well the installation would blend with the pier's existing design and, even, state of disrepair. We found an old, loose pier piling on the eastern side of the pier building and decided to instrument it as a way of observing wave patterns. In the old building, we would most likely take this observation and recreate it so that visitors could twang the pier or generate waves, essentially recreating the forces at play.

"We are driven by as much the emotional impact at times as the educational impact—the way that something feels in a setting or the way that something strikes you is vitally important to the overall experience."

At Fort Mason, we decided to instrument the pier itself. We inserted a bronze rod into the pier and placed a needle into a plate of sand housed in a watertight case. Instead of having visitors recreate the forces, we created an opportunity for visitors to study the complex wave patterns already at play. It was all done very simply, but built like a hardy machine that evokes the history of piers. We call it the "Wave Tracer."

SUSAN   The pier pylon was old and rotting, maybe eighty years old, and then this little piece of machinery was attached to it that was highly refined and even polished. They work together like an odd couple so you really notice how these things are interacting. It makes you want to look over the side of the pier and see what the water's doing, why the waves and the tides are driving this sort of beautiful tracing in the sand.

OPPOSITE The pier at Fort Mason.

SHAWN   The whole point of those pieces was to build pointers to the environment so you would look out and see what was happening. You could actually walk away

RIGHT A close-up of the "Wave Tracer."

from these beautiful objects and tracings in the sand with a way of looking at waves or wind that you could take with you, what we call an "animated aftermath."

EDITOR It's also interesting to hear you say the word beautiful after what we were just talking about—how in the old museum it could appear that nobody cares about how the exhibit looks, but actually you do.

SHAWN Oh, deeply, absolutely. In fact, I think we're driven as much by the beauty of the phenomena as by the content of the piece.

SUSAN For us, it's not about the polish of the beautiful maple wood and the smooth stainless steel knobs. Sometimes the structure around an exhibit dominates a little too much. That's what's really nice about the outdoor pieces—they've simplified the structure so that they focus you on the phenomena. It's a perfection of the ideas we have been using inside. But because the designers had a different set of criteria for outdoor spaces, they made themselves rethink how to design an object that could have an intriguing look, but also have a precise function to connect you to a large-scale phenomenon. This is the aesthetic we've been talking about, it's similar to what artists do. They want to continuously rework an idea, perhaps seeing it differently every time, and to allow the ideas to evolve and grow into something new. Every time they make something they are learning something new about their ideas and that's what a really great exhibit should do, I think.

SHAWN   Yeah, there's a glow of grime. A lot of exhibits are actually built to wear in. They are just beautiful to see with fifteen or twenty years of people tarnish on them. It's kind of a quaint decrepitude; reminds me of New Orleans, where buildings get old with elegance and grace. I like that idea of things being built well—not in that they are highly crafted but they are solid and honest.

SUSAN   You can tell that people enjoy using them over and over and over again.

EDITOR   What do you think Frank Oppenheimer would think about the way exhibit design is evolving in the new space and in the outdoor spaces?

SUSAN   That's a hard question. There are some things we've done that I think he wouldn't like. I wonder what he would have thought about a lot of the visualization technologies we are using now. Computers were beginning to be used a lot before he died, and he thought they would be really great for showing simulations of phenomenon you couldn't see either because they were too big or too small, but he tried to steer us away from doing too much of it or making the exhibits seem like they were too technological. This museum was not supposed to be about technology

BELOW The pier at Fort Mason.

or industry, it was supposed to be about phenomena, connecting people to nature. So, where we have really honed down the apparatus to focus people on a principle of nature, I think he would really approve of that. I think he would have liked the outdoor collection quite a bit.

SHAWN   Working in the state of ambiguity that he encouraged is really tricky. The place was really good at it when Frank was here because there was a kind of playful approach, almost like a jazz musician playing around with an idea or a musical riff. You could argue for this or that, and anything could be okay. That ambiguity is difficult to navigate without a Frank around. When you get second- and third- and fourth-generation people coming in as designers and developers, when you can argue both sides of almost any argument about design, it gets tricky. In some ways you start to wish for a stronger guideline and some constraints.

That's one of the reasons our Fort Mason outdoor project worked so well in the landscape—because we were using the design constraints as both filters and inspiration.

EDITOR   Can you summarize those constraints?

SHAWN   Well, a fundamental constraint was that we were designing installations that encouraged the development of noticing skills. This is very different from building exhibits to function as information delivery devices. Looking at the "Wave Tracer" exhibit, it's just this beautiful machine that encourages you to notice how the wave fronts come from many sources: ship wakes, waves reflecting off the nearby sea wall, waves filtering through the pier pilings. So you develop the noticing skill and how to read the wave patterns and where they come from. We asked ourselves a long list of questions: is it beautiful; is it too ambiguous; is it too full of information so that it becomes overwhelmed with content; does it fit well into the setting; is it aligned with our partners' goals for the park? These were our honing questions; they were constraints in a way but they were also a way of keeping ideas flowing. It made the development process a little bit more rigorous.

SUSAN   We learned so much from Frank. One of the crucial pieces is that, as a working scientist (you know he worked on the Manhattan Project and he was in a laboratory developing prototypes), he knew what it meant to try to understand

"Sometimes the structure around an exhibit dominates a little too much. That's what's really nice about the outdoor pieces—they've simplified the structure so that they focus you on the phenomena. It's a perfection of the ideas we have been using inside."

a process through prototype development. So what has happened is that exhibits actually look a lot less like prototypes than they used to. We have become more sensitive to the public. We want to make sure things are safe to use and that they are accessible to everyone. We have a professional research and evaluation department (not the exhibit developer) who tests new ideas and exhibits with the public. They make sure the graphics work, that everyone understands how to use the exhibit. Every new exhibit now goes through an evaluation criteria. The research and evaluation team works with the exhibit developer, so the developer also feels that the final exhibit communicates the things that got them interested in investigating that particular phenomena in the first place.

SHAWN   Our evaluation team has gotten more and more sophisticated in the way that they assess exhibits. Of course, informal evaluation has always been a part of Exploratorium design process. Designers always talk to staff and visitors as a way of iteratively prototyping an idea. I think the thing that sets the Exploratorium apart, still, is our sense of fearlessness when we're developing exhibits—you just want to do what's right for the piece and for the visitor and for yourself. Whatever gets between you and that goal needs to be moved over, gone under or through. That sense of passion and focus is at the heart of what we do. The character of the new location will be driven by this more than anything else.

The Evolution of an Exhibit

Excerpts from an article published twenty-five years ago. By Pat Murphy

Frank Oppenheimer believed that no exhibit could ever be considered complete; if a change could improve the exhibit, then the change should be made. This attitude has shaped the process of exhibit development at the Exploratorium. Here, exhibit development is an evolutionary process, involving prolonged experimentation and tinkering. In fact, exhibit design and exhibit construction are often so intertwined that it's difficult to say where one leaves off and the other begins.

Few exhibits emerge from our machine shop fully formed. Most evolve over time, shaped by the ideas of the exhibit builder and staff and the reactions of visitors. In a sense, all the exhibits at the Exploratorium—even ones that have been on display for years—are prototypes. The never-ending mutation of exhibits can be a source of frustration (won't this exhibit ever be done?) and delight (think how much better it will work if we just do this!).

As director, Frank established the museum's broad pedagogical structure. To a first-time visitor, the Exploratorium may seem chaotic. But Frank perceived an underlying sense of unity that emerged from the conceptual interconnections among exhibits rather than from superficial uniformity of appearance or exhibit style. He wrote, "In the minds of those who have conceived, fabricated, and assembled the exhibits, the Exploratorium is a very structured environment. We are careful not to impose any behaviour patterns or learning strategies on our visitors. At first some visitors are a little upset. They ask: 'Where shall we begin?' In the end, all manner of people discover how to use this place. We observe that they use it in many different ways and for a great variety of purposes."

More often than not, Frank was involved in every stage of an exhibit's development—from the first mention of the idea to the never-ending fine tuning of the exhibit on the museum floor. Sometimes he built exhibits himself, humming as he worked in the machine shop, wearing, as always, a suit and tie. (Staff members remember watching and wondering when Frank would catch his dangling tie in the lathe—but he never did.) Frank also often suggested exhibit ideas to others, never assigning the project, but attempting to drum up interest. "I have this idea," he would say. "Would you be interested in working on it?"

The willingness of the Exploratorium staff to tinker around with things also reflects Frank's influence. One staff member recalls, "He would encourage people to just go off and really develop their ideas and explore and fiddle with things. He was really good at allowing that kind of fiddling and tinkering time."

In writing about teaching, Frank expressed the opinion that the best teacher was, "someone who, having enjoyed learning something, eagerly wants to communicate it to others." At the Exploratorium, it is the people who are intrigued and excited by the phenomena to be displayed who design the exhibits—and also construct and refine, study the reaction of visitors, decide to make improvements or changes.

Many Exploratorium exhibits grow out of a staff member's interest in a particular natural phenomenon or scientific principle. Others emerge from the teaching kits developed by Exploratorium staff members. A number of exhibits at the Exploratorium can better be described as art pieces than as science exhibits.

In every case, exhibit development at the Exploratorium involves a great deal of play, learn-

ABOVE Frank Oppenheimer plays with Bob Miller's "Distilled Light" exhibit. Photo by Nancy Rodger © Exploratorium

ing, discussion, experimentation, and tinkering. Each exhibit develops in a different way, shaped by the interests and idiosyncrasies of the exhibit builder, the reactions of the staff and visitors.

The Exploratorium has no structural style to which exhibits must conform: the museum makes no attempt to dictate exhibit size, colour, or shape. The look of an exhibit is dictated by its function and by the builder's preferences, so they can each look quite different. However, there are some general principles and characteristics that apply to almost all the exhibits developed at the Exploratorium.

General principle and characteristics of exhibit design

- *Basic research—just plain tinkering around with something for the fun of it—is an essential part of the exhibit development process.* At the Exploratorium, approximately four-fifths of the cost of an exhibit is in the research and design, and only one-fifth is in the final construction.

- *Exhibits are designed and developed by people who are interested in the phenomenon to be displayed.* If the exhibit builder doesn't enjoy the exhibit and want to show it to other people, the exhibit is less likely to be successful. Often, the same person (or people) conceives of, designs, and constructs the exhibit.

- *To some extent, all exhibits are collaborative: many people make suggestions and contribute ideas.* We have found that it's important to involve a diverse group of people, including artists and teachers, as well as scientists and engineers.

- *The first stage of exhibit design is the construction of a full-scale working prototype.* Reactions to the prototype help the exhibit builder modify and improve the exhibit. The final version of the exhibit is often built around the material in the prototype. As a result, the nature and size of the exhibit are dictated by functional considerations and the phenomenon to be displayed.

- *Exhibit builders are responsive to comments from visitors and staff, testing exhibits at many stages in their development and allowing reactions to shape the exhibit.* But at the same time, exhibit builders try to please themselves, constructing an exhibit that communicates their own excitement about a particular phenomenon.

- *Exhibit builders pay attention to aesthetic nuances, noticing what is fun to do, what is beautiful, what is intriguing.* Each exhibit has its own aesthetic of some sort—visual, tactile, scientific.

- *Generally, exhibit builders try not to restrict a visitor's choices.* Rather than just providing one thing for a visitor to try, an exhibit may give a visitor a few options, allowing room for experimentation and play.

- *Ideally, visitors should be able to see the inner workings of an exhibit and make discoveries about how the exhibit works.* Usually, exhibits are built in a simple fashion to help visitors feel that they could, if they wanted, try the same thing at home.

OPPOSITE An Exploratorium visitor interacts with Ned Kahn's "Tornado" exhibit. Photo by Nancy Rodger © Exploratorium

THIS PAGE Artist-in-residence Ned Kahn continuing to develop the "Tornado" exhibit in the Exploratorium's Machine Shop. Photo by Susan Schwartzenberg © Exploratorium

- *Most exhibits are set up on tabletops, so that visitors can gather and use the exhibit together.* This arrangement encourages visitors to watch other people use exhibits and promotes social interaction between visitors.

- *Exhibits are often constructed of inexpensive materials, scrap, and found objects (or junk).* As a result, an exhibit can be changed readily without much expense.

- *Almost all of the Exploratorium's exhibits are built at the museum.* This allows museum staff to interact with the exhibit builder and the exhibit, and makes it easy to test the exhibit on the museum floor, a crucial stage in its development.

Of course, these are guidelines, not absolute rules. Though they describe our general approach to exhibit development, we could probably find successful Exploratorium exhibits that contradict each of them. In the end, we try to build exhibits that please our visitors as well as ourselves, to listen to comments, and always, to be willing to change.

E very year, in his role as chair of the Banff Science
Communications program, Jay Ingram gives a
public talk. For this volume, he has prepared an
article based on one of those talks. Also included, in the
sidebar, is an explanation of how he came up with the
presentation version of this same topic. Together, the article
and the sidebar show how audience and setting strongly
influence the way you tell a great science story. Ingram is a
science writer and broadcaster who has been the host of a
television show on Discovery Channel in Canada for fifteen
years. He is the author of eleven popular books on science.

Watson and Crick, Lennon and McCartney: Creativity and Collaboration

Jay Ingram

Scientists know that creativity is an essential part of the scientific process. Non-scientists often don't know this, familiar only with the rigid formula they learned in Grade Eight for doing science—objective, materials, method. No room for creative thinking there.

How wrong could this be? It is hard to define creativity, but it's also obvious that science icons like Newton, Darwin, and Einstein weren't just collecting information and coming up with predictable conclusions: they were way out beyond that.

Maybe the notion of the solitary genius hides the fact that a lot of the creative work in science occurs between people. Creativity happens between people in ways we can't see. I'm going to make the case that this mysterious process goes on in both art and science. But first, are there other similarities?

Newton is most famous for deriving a theory of gravity from the incident of the falling apple, but this bare-bones telling of the story ignores the crucial part: that he, the great, great genius, drew a parallel between the apple's fall and the orbit of the moon. Darwin might have begun the voyage of the *Beagle* simply gathering data, but in the end, the story he told is still making waves today. And Einstein, of course, was able to create a new vision of space and time by thinking hard.

All three of these examples suggest that, at least when it comes to science, imagination plays a critical role. There are spaces in our understanding of nature, and, occasionally, questioning minds are able to fill in parts of them.

But, skeptics say, this is a completely different thing than artistic creativity, where the artist invents—or creates—a vision and realizes it. That vision did not exist before that artist, whereas space-time, evolution, and gravity have always been there, waiting for someone to discover them.

But that is not as straightforward or ironclad an argument as it seems. When you take into account the uncertainty that plagues even the hardest science, physics, it's clear that while there might be things we can discover, certainty is always just out of reach. As a result, at each stage in the development of a science, researchers create a view of the world that is consistent with the data (the data they choose to include, at any rate). Even when there is something near certainty, as when Watson and Crick figured out the structure of DNA, some observers maintained that it was crucial for the development of biology that it was Watson and Crick who delivered the verdict with such aplomb.

Anyone else, Nobelist Sir Peter Medawar claimed, "then it would still have been a great episode in biological history; but something more in the common run of things; something splendidly well done, but not in the grand romantic manner."[1] When the expression of the idea is the thing that sets it apart, you could be describing a great work of fiction.

Does the creative work, whatever it is, stand out from all the rest? Does it advance the field? Is it truly beautiful? All of these statements apply to both art and science: "beautiful" solutions to scientific problems have always had more appeal to scientists than routine or even clumsy ones. Both art and science are limited by the available technology; both are confined by schools of thought and/or stylistic convention.

However, it is as important to admit the differences as it is to promote the similarities. It is true that the arrow that defines the direction of the creative process appears to point in opposite directions for artists and scientists. Scientists are usually trying to narrow down the possibilities, converging on a solution that is the best answer to a problem, whereas the artist is realizing an inner vision that may start with a sketch, but then morph into something else that, in the beginning, might not have even been imagined.

The science arrow might find the mark, but where does that artistic arrow land? It may be that a final product is never achieved. After fifty-five hours of studio time, the Beatles settled on the final version of "Strawberry Fields Forever," but John Lennon, the man who wrote and sang it, still wasn't satisfied. Michelangelo left three-fifths of his sculptures unfinished, not because of missed deadlines or lack of funding, but, as neurobiologist Semir Zeki puts it, "Michelangelo realized the hopelessness of translating into a single work or a series of sculptures the synthetic ideals formed in his brain."[2]

A scientist, on the other hand, might well have "synthetic ideals" in his or her mind, but if they aren't realized, it will indeed be lack of funding that curtails his or her pursuit. So scientists ask questions that they think are answerable, given the technology and expertise at hand. Unrealistic just doesn't get done.

Is this a creative cop-out? Does this constraint of asking questions that likely have answers forever limit creativity? You would think so: how could you be giving free rein to your imagination if you have to limit the questions you ask and the approach you take? But therein lies the creative opportunity: the chance to ask brilliant—but practical—questions of nature. Questions that are likely to yield answers.

Of all the examples I've referenced so far, my favourites are Watson and Crick, and Lennon and McCartney. None appear in the upper echelons of creative figures like Mozart, Beethoven, Newton, or Einstein. But they nevertheless represent to me beautiful examples of how the creative act usually happens—by groups of individuals, contributing in myriad ways.

Watson and Crick's 1953 DNA discovery, and their subsequent Nobel Prizes, weren't particularly controversial until James Watson published his gossip-guy memoir of the whole affair. He was so dismissive of Rosalind Franklin, a rival at King's College, London, that rumours grew that Watson had stolen an important X-ray image of DNA from her lab. Although it hadn't been theft, the image was the key piece of evidence Watson and Crick needed to complete their picture of DNA. In fact, they happily admitted that Franklin's image—and some other information about DNA she had supplied to a departmental document that somehow found its way into W and C's hands (again, apparently legitimately)—dominated their thinking as they closed in on the structure.

Even at the last minute, outsiders intervened in the creative process. On the crucial Saturday in their lab at Cambridge, a physical chemist named Jerry Donohue looked on as Watson shuffled molecular models around, trying to get these particular building blocks to fit together neatly into the DNA superstructure. Donohue pointed out that Watson was using the wrong versions of the molecules. Watson came back with the irrefutable fact that these were the versions in the textbook. But, countered Donohue, everyone knew those were incorrect. Correcting them set Watson on his way to the final assembly of DNA.

The discovery had the fingerprints of others all over it. But no one was more important to Watson and Crick than Watson and Crick. They did virtually no experimentation; instead, they read, and talked, and thought, and talked some more. They threw out crazy ideas, and were never reluctant to brand them as crazy. Crick maintained that rudeness was essential to good science. They were under pressure: just down the road Franklin and Maurice Wilkins were nibbling at DNA; the genius of molecular structure at Caltech, Linus Pauling, had blown one attempt at the structure, and wasn't likely to make that mistake again. But the pressure simply fed into their confidence and competitiveness. Watson and Crick were both smart, but in different ways, with different areas of expertise. Crick claimed that without Watson, he would never have discovered DNA. But they were together, and he did.

A decade later, in 1963, Lennon and McCartney were on their way to the "toppermost of the poppermost." Three years after that, they had become the greatest pop group of all time. The key ingredient in that greatness was the songwriting of Lennon and McCartney, although by 1966 the two were struggling to get along, and much of their collaboration—if you could call it that—was separate, not together.

In the fall of 1966, Lennon was in the south of Spain, acting in a Richard Lester film called *How I Won the*

Does the creative work, whatever it is, stand out from all the rest? Does it advance the field? Is it truly beautiful?

War. It was there he began to put together "It's Not Too Bad," a mournful, inward-looking song that signalled an awareness that he was different than most and expressed it with a mix of clarity and indifference, all filtered through the fog of too much LSD. Lennon's first recordings of the song are hesitant and erratic, but he kept at it, and began to give the song some shape once back at his home studio outside London. It was now called "Strawberry Fields Forever."

But here's the thing. It wasn't until he brought this skeleton of a song into the studio, and began to collaborate, that it became something significant. It wasn't just that his band mates were the Beatles (although what other band would have added instruments like Paul's Mellotron or George's swarmandel?) but that his producer was George Martin. While I like to compare the creative efforts of the two musicians to the two scientists, there was no equivalent of George Martin for Watson and Crick.

Here is just one piece of supporting evidence: after more than two dozen takes of "Strawberry Fields Forever," Lennon told Martin that he liked the beginning of Take 7 and the rest of Take 26, and could George simply put them together. Martin pointed out that they had been recorded at different tempi and in different keys, so just splicing them wouldn't work. Lennon insisted. So Martin slowed down one take, speeded up the other, and they matched. The final version of "Strawberry Fields Forever" is indeed the spliced version. The edit is at the one-minute mark, the abrupt entrance of trumpets and cellos (that George Martin scored) turning the song much, much darker.

Neither W and C nor L and M could have reached their respective pinnacles of creativity without the input of many others. Nor can that input be narrowly defined as bits of scientific data or actual musical phrases. There was pressure: Watson and Crick were pushed by their rivals, but so were the Beatles. The Beach Boys' Brian Wilson had promised to answer the Beatles' last work with an opus of his own, and they were well aware of his enormous talent. He was their Linus Pauling.

Both partnerships built on what others had achieved, although with constraints. The Beatles had to sell records; W and C had to operate within the canon of chemistry. They both made brutal mistakes: Watson and Crick constructed a chemically naive structure for DNA that Rosalind Franklin was able to dismiss at a glance, and anyone who has watched the execrable *Magical Mystery Tour* knows that the Beatles unleashed were just a bunch of amateur moviemakers.

And again, each member of the pair influenced the other. I've already outlined the peculiar and unique teamwork of W and C; in the Beatles' case, even though by 1966 that influence was often malign (Lennon was sure that McCartney didn't take "Strawberry Fields Forever" seriously), it was effective. Each curbed the other's worst excesses.

So where exactly is the creative act in this welter of people, technology, and ideas? First, there is no doubt that the central figures in these stories are the creators. However haphazard and unpolished the earliest recordings of "Strawberry Fields Forever" are compared to the final product, the emotion of the song is John Lennon's. Similarly, while W and C didn't hesitate to use Rosalind Franklin's data, it was they who put it all together. She might have been no more than two steps away from the double helix, but she never got there.

However, identifying the creators is much easier than pinpointing the creative act, and there is a simple reason for that. If you accumulate all the available evidence about creativity, from personal testimony to lab experiments, the single feature that stands out is that creativity is unconscious. Great creative moments do not result from computer-like idea crunching; they arrive out of the blue.

William Blake is only one of many artists and scientists who have recognized this in themselves, but he put it very well:

I have written this poem from immediate dictation, twelve or sometimes twenty or thirty lines at a time without premeditation, and even against my will. The time it has taken in writing was thus rendered non-existent, and an immense poem exists produced without labour or study.[3]

On a much more mundane level, psychologists trying to entrap creativity in the lab are reduced to putting subjects in an fMRI and showing them something called a Remote Associates Test. The subjects are given three words—pine, crab, sauce—and are asked to find a word that can be paired with all of them.[4]

Sometimes the discovery of that word can be what the psychologists call an "aha" moment: you don't arrive at the answer by grinding your way through the alphabet, it simply hits you. Out of nowhere. By associating the subject's claim of an "aha" moment with the patterns of brain activation in the fMRI, some—very tentative—conclusions can be drawn about what happens in the brain at these moments, and where. What these studies suggest is that there are indeed changing patterns of activity prior to the "aha" moment, but the subject is unaware of them.

These studies are by no means replications of great moments of creativity, but they are consistent with the idea that preparing the ground for such creativity takes place outside one's awareness. In the same way, I don't think Watson, Crick, Lennon, or McCartney could have pinpointed when or how their brilliant ideas came to fruition—they just did.

In the end, the unconscious must be the feature that fundamentally links artistic and scientific creativity. It will also be the one that frustrates those who try to define the process in either group.

In the end, as Francis Crick put it, quoting the painter John Minton: "The important thing is to be there when the picture is painted."[5]

1 In "Lucky Jim," a review of James Watson's book *The Double Helix*, by Sir Peter Medawar in the *New York Review of Books*, March 28, 1968.

2 Samir Zeki, "Artistic Creativity and the Brain," *Science*, no. 5527 (July 6, 2001): 51–2.

3 Letter to Thomas Butts, April 25, 1803, regarding his poem "Jerusalem" in *The Letters of William Blake*, edited by Geoffrey Keynes (London: MacMillan, 1956), p. 85.

4 The answer is "apple."

5 Francis Crick, *What Mad Pursuit: A Personal View of Scientific Discovery* (New York: Basic Books, 1990), p. 78.

Start with the T-shirt

Jay Ingram

I wanted to prepare an engaging public talk on Watson and Crick, Lennon and McCartney. There is something really interesting about creativity in these star collaborations to which I knew an audience would be able to relate.

Presenting this topic as a public lecture has its risks: two-thirds of the audience (at least) will have no clue that Watson and Crick discovered DNA (or know what DNA even is); two-thirds of the audience will likely have been born after the Beatles broke up.

So, I started in the logical place: I developed a tour T-shirt. Then, I got my hands on two fantastic pieces around which such a talk can be built.

One is an amazing animation showing how Rosalind Franklin's Photo 51, an historically significant image that is meaningless at first glance, reveals the DNA double helix—at least if you know what to look for. My animation is unique: it was created by Alex Tirabasso at the Canadian Museum of Nature in Gatineau. It takes you through each feature of the critical black-and-white image, and makes sense of it. It's

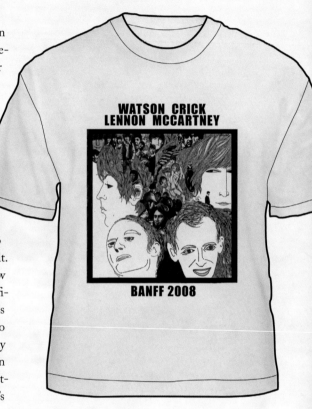

one thing to say that Photo 51 was crucial; it's quite another to see what it is that scientists were seeing for the first time.

On the arts side, I had a remarkable archive of numerous takes of "Strawberry Fields Forever," starting with John Lennon playing the song alone in Spain and ending with the famous splice of Take 7 and Take 26 from studio recordings in London. Simply playing crucial takes from this series builds the song from a simplistic strum to one of the greatest pop songs of all time.

If you have the animation and the song archive in hand, you can build the story around them. I begin by using multiple images of DNA, each slightly more realistic than the last, to get the audience familiar with how it is put together. Once they know that, and understand the laboratory social interactions involving Watson, Crick, and their rivals, the audience is ready for the photo that changed the world. The story turns around it.

"Strawberry Fields Forever" is not pivotal in the same way, but it beautifully illustrates some of the parallels between the two pairs of creators. And, it brings audio very naturally into a public science talk.

I've gotten into trouble before for saying this, but at least in this instance, one's reaction to the song is almost purely emotional; the reaction to the DNA double helix, not so much. Satisfying, intriguing, even promising, but not deeply emotional. I've gotten into trouble from scientists who argue that science is indeed emotional, and while I agree with them generally, I feel that in this case there is a sharp difference.

Having visuals that solve a science mystery and a soundtrack that sweeps you up are ingredients for a public talk about science and creativity that can be emotional and engaging. Yes, a science talk.

Tracy Day is an Emmy Award–winning documentary producer and the executive producer of the World Science Festival, which she co-founded with husband, Brian Greene, a well-known physicist and author of several books on science. In an exclusive interview with Jay Ingram for this book, she talks about the inspiration for the festival, an annual June event that started in 2008 and now attracts well over a hundred thousand viewers each year. The festival has been described as a tribute to imagination, ingenuity, and inventiveness, and takes science out of the laboratory and into the streets, theatres, museums, and public halls of New York City.

On Centre Stage: The Greatest Adventure Story on Earth

Jay Ingram interviews Tracy Day

JAY   Where did the idea for the World Science Festival come from?

TRACY Well, two answers to that. I'll give you the "aha" moment and then the lead up to it. The "aha" moment was when we were having a dinner in New York with Vittorio Bo, whom you may know from the Genoa Science Festival in Italy which had just started the year before. He had come to New York to talk to Brian about that. I was sort of dragged along to the dinner as the wife, and I had just had a baby and I had finished up projects from ABC and wasn't really focused on next projects, but as he spoke, Brian and I at the same time thought, well this is interesting, does anything like this exist in America?

We realized that there are science fairs, which are high-school displays of experiments, etcetera, but nothing that resembled the kind of thing that Vittorio was talking about. It became one of those moments where you realize what a natural and wonderful event it would be. And it tapped into what we both did in a sense. I'm a producer. I was a producer at ABC News, so my background is really taking non-fiction content and bringing it to a large audience. Brian is a scientist who does this too.

So that was the "aha" moment and we moved very quickly on it because we just loved the idea and couldn't stop thinking about it and couldn't stop the brainstorming and such.

The lead up to it, for me anyway, was that being in broadcasting we never did science. We never went there at all and I started to discover through various projects how fascinating and varied the content was and how it wasn't really brought to a general audience in a way that was as compelling as the material itself. Brian and I met on an ABC project called *The Century*. The final segment was called "The Thinkers." I interviewed a number of extraordinary people and they were as compelling and interesting as anyone. Brian happened to be one of them and the story goes on! So that was the lead up I had as a producer to realizing there's an audience for science out there and they're underserved and you can have so much creative fun with the material.

JAY   One of the big differences between a festival and the media is that the festival is "in person"—people go and attend events. In that sense, it's unlike TV or radio. What was so attractive about the live medium?

TRACY   It had life. We decided that we're going to do these events in theatres, not in lecture halls. We're going to produce them with the same discipline and understanding of how you take intellectual content and bring it to a live audience, whether it's live by a broadcast or live in a theatre, so that you know exactly where it's going. You have a narrative, you use multimedia, you have a kind of disciplined approach as opposed to a chat with interesting people, and you walk into the theatre and the lights go down so the message immediately is, "this is a performance." It's intellectual content, but it's a performance and you're going to be moved, we hope, intellectually and emotionally, and be excited.

JAY   Do you ban PowerPoint?

TRACY   It depends on how one defines PowerPoint. People don't come and give their PowerPoints; that's not why they're invited. It's not what we do. Some of it may be projected using that technical tool, though.

JAY   You mentioned that you want to excite people both intellectually and emotionally and, for my money, the second of those two might be the most important. What do you think?

TRACY   I completely agree and it's very important for people who are a bit afraid of science, or for those to whom it wouldn't occur to go to a science event, to be first of all excited and enticed by the topic and then to go there and have an experience that hits them in a place other than the intellect. It's very, very powerful and it's not easy.
    A striking example of that was our opening at Alice Tully Hall at Lincoln Center. It was a performing-arts salute to science and it was in honour of Ian Wilson. So, first of all, we wanted a program that was worthy of Lincoln Center—so that it measured up on the cultural side as well as being true to what we do, which is bring science to a general audience. Some of the components were Yo-Yo Ma playing Bach to little kids from the National Dance Institute, which is a public school program here in New York. The kids are not dancers, but they learn to dance. They were dancing ants. They danced around Yo-Yo Ma. Brian Greene and Joshua Bell did a kind of duet where Joshua played and Brian would take the audience on a tour of the universe with multimedia components. There was a full orchestra that was performing a Phillip Glass piece with beautiful visuals shot by *National Geographic*

photographer Frans Lanting. By the end of that, there were people in the audience in tears. What a strange thing that is. It's a science event and it had touched people in a way that you wouldn't expect a science event to do. So that was rewarding.

JAY   From what you've said so far, it sounds to me like one of the most important features is to make it clear that it's a performance and not a lecture.

TRACY   Right—without ignoring the fact that this is about serious science. It's not serious science in what we used to call the "eat your peas approach"—that is, this is important, therefore, you must know it and pay attention to it. It's more showcasing that science is the ultimate adventure story. This content doesn't need candy coating—you don't have to mask the science to reach a public audience. What you have to do is release it so they see the excitement of it. On its own merit, it opens their minds. There's a recognition that it permeates their lives and it's extraordinary. It's not work when it's presented that way.

JAY   The festival has a large number of different kinds of presentations. If you had to isolate one or two that you thought were the most successful, what would they be?

TRACY   You know, the reason there's a range is because we recognize that we're tapping into different audiences, and different audiences have different tastes. So a hardcore science audience may be interested in some of the higher-level science programs in the festival, *The Parallel Worlds* or *The Theory of Nothing*, *The Biological Biography*. Some people are going to be attracted to that and they want a straightforward presentation, but again, produced in a sense that we take great pains to not just put people on a stage and say, ready, set, go talk.

   The art-science programs are more unique. They're also, in a way more, dangerous. A lot of times when you try to do an art-science mix you sort of bring both down, so it's difficult. The mix has to be organic; it cannot be contrived. The program cannot be an art program where you then step out and do a pedagogical presentation of science. So it's the trickiest, but I think it's the thing that people have found very exciting.

JAY   You have had what anybody would say is an all-star lineup of scientists, but not just great scientists, great science communicators. Is that pool limited?

TRACY   I don't think so. I think some people are more natural than others, but I think there's a huge range of scientists at various levels and at various stages of their careers who can communicate well. I think we tapped into a change in the scientific community. I think that they want to communicate. Not too long ago, scientists seemed not to have much interest in communicating to a lay audience in language other than the scientific jargon, which is, of course, the language of science that many people don't understand. They're afraid that if they step out of that it somehow dumbs down the science. I think that's changed. I think that more scientists are willing to entertain different ways to communicate science to the public other than their standard PowerPoint. And one of the things we want to do is have this be a platform for really fine science communication and for scientists to feel rewarded for that and recognized for that.

JAY   If you could look back from some point in the future and say we actually moved scientists, or a significant number of them, in that direction toward better communication, that would be a singular achievement.

TRACY   That's right, and it is one of the goals, absolutely, and we are discovering extraordinary people and we look for them, actively look for them.

JAY   What has surprised you the most?

TRACY   I guess what surprised me the most is the very thing we had hoped for, which is an unexpected broader audience becoming engaged and excited about science. We thought it was there—otherwise we wouldn't have bothered to do this—but you don't know until you do it.
     One of the events is a family street fair on the weekend. Brian and I stood there and looked out at over a hundred thousand people gathered. The excitement there was palpable. At some of the events in the theatre it felt like you were at a Broadway opening, it had that kind of energy. The diversity of the audience was incredible: age, scientific knowledge, background, race, gender—it was startling. All of the programs sold out. People would show up hoping to buy tickets that become available at the last minute. There would be a big long lineup outside, like going to a rock concert!

JAY   Were there scalpers?

TRACY   There were actually at the Lincoln Center event, it was very funny.

JAY   Do you think this would work in a city other than New York?

TRACY   Yes, I do, but the character of the festival really does needs to align with where it's happening. So you would take a good hard look at where you are doing this and figure out what is special there and how you do a festival such as this.

JAY   Let's face it: it requires inspired and inspirational people and with you and Brian, I think, you can't deny that was a key part. We run a science communication workshop for two weeks at The Banff Centre and one of our favourite sayings to people who come in and seem a little bit blocked in terms of wanting to step outside and really communicate science in different ways, is that the only reason we're not doing it is that we're not doing it. I think that you and Brian have shown that you can do it.

TRACY   Well, that's part of it too; it just made so much sense to us. I hate to sound naive and silly but it's just so cool for me as an outsider in science, it's just so fascinating, and Brian of course knew that already. He had already seen the impact of communicating science to a general audience, what can happen on the stage with an audience. It's very gratifying.

JAY   You and Brian are a couple and you are also the collaborators. How does that work?

TRACY   A friend of ours who runs another festival warned us that this will take over our life and I can confirm in many ways it has. You know that when your four-year-old answers the phone, "World Science Festival, can I help you?"! In fact, it works incredibly well because, number one, we tend to see the potential of this in very similar ways and, also, we bring very different things to it, very different backgrounds. I'm not a scientist, he's not a producer, just that alone makes it work, so you're not in each other's turf, in a sense, but also we just work well together. Of course, one would never know before you did it, so it's a very high-stakes game.

JAY   You're courageous in both senses, not only to inaugurate the festival but to do it with Brian. Just one final question: What could people who work in the area of communicating science learn from your experiences of the World Science Festival?

TRACY   I think that they can learn that they can communicate science without being afraid of the science. That they shouldn't try to mask it or dumb it down. They should have faith in the material. They should be willing to not stick to the safe way of communicating, which is again by a PowerPoint or the kind of familiar presentations that one uses effectively within the science community. Go outside, have fun with it, recognize that the stories are wonderful.

IF TV SCIENCE WAS MORE LIKE REAL SCIENCE

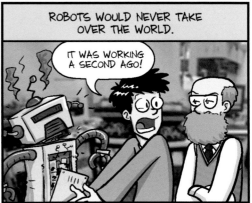

WWW.PHDCOMICS.COM

UK *science writer and broadcaster Simon Singh answered a few questions for this volume about his work on preparing science talks for the stage. His project, Theatre of Science, aims "to make science a hot night out by presenting humorous and thought-provoking lectures in a theatrical space." He is a columnist, television broadcaster, and the author of numerous books, including* Big Bang, The Code Book, *and* Fermat's Last Theorem, *a topic he also covered in a BBC television documentary. His latest book,* Trick or Treatment? Alternative Medicine on Trial, *was co-authored with Edzard Ernst. Singh holds a Ph.D. in physics, and is a frequent commentator on science.*

Science on Stage

Interview with Simon Singh

EDITOR When you were working on your Ph.D. in physics, how much room was there for creativity in your academic presentations?

SIMON Science lectures to fellow academics are there to communicate information, or to encourage debate, or to argue a case, as opposed to public lectures, which also have the function to stimulate interest and perhaps entertain. Hence, the former tends to be lacking in creativity and the latter benefits hugely from creativity. However, I find that I have lectured to many different audiences and in each case I have learned techniques that have been enhanced by my overall ability to communicate science—starting with presenting during my Ph.D., to tutoring undergraduates, teaching schoolchildren, radio interviews, TV interviews, TV directing, TV and radio broadcasting, public lectures, theatre lectures, and so on.

EDITOR What are you trying to accomplish with science on stage?

SIMON My colleague Richard Wiseman and I wanted to see if it was possible to present our normal lectures in a theatre context and attract a new audience. We did tweak our material, reorder it, recast it, and market it in a different way, but essentially we were going to present ideas that we had already talked about. As well as attracting a new audience, the plan was also to encourage others to experiment with this idea and to grab press attention. An indirect effect was that it led to new ideas, which in turn had many spinoffs. For example, the show started in London and then went to the Edinburgh Fringe Festival and then to an off-Broadway theatre in New York, and it also led to a TV program.

EDITOR Why is humour so important, especially with live audiences?

SIMON .I think humour is important because it varies the pace of the lecture and makes the whole experience more enjoyable. Teenagers who may be scared of physics suddenly begin to like the lecturer, and if they begin to like the messenger then they are more likely to be interested in the message. There are many opportunities for humour, because science can be so weird. Scientists do strange things to find out even stranger things. I think the key point is not to aim to be relentlessly funny, but to deliver the lecture and to then look for opportunities when humour emerges naturally. The humour should be seen as bonus, albeit a very welcome one. Often I have given a talk and the audience has laughed at a very unexpected moment, so the next time I gave that lecture I made sure to include that phrasing or diagram and to play up the previously unanticipated humorous aspect.

EDITOR   How important, to you, is it to take risks in science communications?

SIMON   Once I start to develop a talk, I try to present it several times, honing it and adding to it each time. I have to give a talk at least half a dozen times before I am happy with it, and even then it will continue to evolve. It is important to take risks, but if I try something out for the first time then I will embed it within something that I know is fairly reliable. This means that if the experimental section is a disaster then I know that I have something to help me recover.

EDITOR   You don't often see science presentations billed as fresh and shocking, the way yours are. Why is that?

SIMON   I don't think my talks are particularly fresh or shocking. In fact, I think presenters often try too hard to be innovative, either with radical formats or new technology. I firmly believe that a traditional talk, well-structured and presented with enthusiasm, is the most effective way to communicate science. Just make sure that the content is interesting and entertaining, and then allow plenty of time for questions at the end.

EDITOR   Why are you so passionate about science and taking it to the public?

"I have derived so much pleasure from science that I want others to experience that same thrill of discovery."

SIMON   I love science and wish I could have been a scientist. However, my talents lay in communicating science so I pursued a career in that direction, whether it is in radio, TV, print, or live presentations. I have derived so much pleasure from science that I want others to experience that same thrill of discovery. Increasingly, I am concerned that the general public needs to be scientifically literate in order to make good judgments in our scientific age. Whereas in the past I would have concentrated on mathematics and cosmology, I am now also touching on the evidence for climate change and the lack of evidence for so many alternative therapies.

EDITOR   Does it take courage to do what you do?

SIMON   I don't think that being a good science presenter can in any way be described as courageous. Instead, one of the most important qualities is the ability to scrutinize every aspect of a lecture in order to improve it. Self-criticism is crucial if a presenter is going to improve content and delivery. I encourage others to point out flaws in a talk, but often people are unwilling to be brutally honest or are unable to give the required level of detail, so a friend whom you can trust and whose opinion you trust can be a valuable asset.

Duncan Dallas is a science communicator who started the Café Scientifique movement when he organized the first Café in Leeds in the U.K. in 1998. There are now Science Cafés in hundreds of major cities around the world. Often, these are partnerships that involve the local university and science centre, but anyone can start one. Café Scientifique is a grassroots movement with some particularly noteworthy features from a science communications perspective: it engages scientists from all areas of research, meets the public where they live, and does not require that scientists have particularly strong communications skills. In this article—which began as a talk to the American Association for the Advancement of Science (AAAS) conference in St. Louis in February 2006 and has been updated for this volume—Dallas explains how the idea got started and why he thinks it has spread so readily. A checklist for starting your own Science Café is included.

Café Scientifique

Duncan Dallas

Café Scientifique is the first worldwide network devoted to publicly discussing science. It is expanding fast at a time when the discussion of science is starting to be almost as important as science itself. There are now well over 250 Cafés in more than forty countries holding regular events. At a time when science depends not just on government funding, but also on public support, Café Scientifique is one type of public engagement with science that, as the science magazine Nature has commented, is bound to grow over the next decade.

A Café Scientifique is defined as "a place where, for the price of a cup of coffee or a glass of wine, people meet to discuss the latest ideas of science and technology which are changing our lives." Its unique selling point turns out to be that changing the location of discussion changes the agenda, tone, and nature of the debate. In a lecture hall, you expect to be lectured to. In a café, you expect to have a conversation. The aim of the Cafés is to bring science into conversation and back into our culture.

For too long science has been seen as a self-defining, self-motivating, self-regulating discipline deciding its own goals and agenda with little reference to the rest of culture. This is clearly no longer the case, and the more science permeates our daily lives, bringing with it both benefits and problems, the more it needs to be debated, discussed, questioned, and examined publicly. The Cafés provide one such forum.

How did it all start?

In 1998, I was reading the obituary of Marc Sautet, founder of the Café Philosophique movement in France. He was a philosopher who had failed to interest the business community in philosophy so he developed the idea of open, free, and public discussion in cafés. I knew that several Cafés Philosophiques had been tried in England but had not taken off. I suspected that was because the Anglo-Saxons considered philosophy a wacky continental subject not to be taken seriously. However, I knew that the English take science seriously and that offered the basis for some interest. I glanced up from the newspaper and right across the

"In a café, you expect to have a conversation. The aim of the Cafés is to bring science into conversation and back into our culture."

way was a small café/bar that was normally closed on Mondays. The owner agreed to open up for one night; I rang a local academic who had written a newspaper article criticizing Richard Dawkins for *The Selfish Gene*, put a poster in the window of the café, told some friends, and crossed my fingers.

Although I would have been happy if a dozen interested people had turned up, in fact over thirty came. But as the speaker started to talk, my heart sank to my boots; he talked in academic jargon, as though addressing students. Fortunately, after his twenty minute talk, we had to have a break for drinks, as the coffee machine had been turned off during the talk because it was too noisy. After this break, once the audience started to ask questions, the evening improved rapidly. The speaker began to realize who he was talking to and what he had to explain. The questions were simple, direct, and often difficult, and the speaker began to think on his feet, always an enjoyable spectacle for the audience. So, the evening was a modest success.

I organized another one, also well attended, and what surprised me then was that people kept coming up to me and asking when the next one was and how much they were looking forward to it. It slowly dawned on me that I had accidentally discovered a real appetite for science and discussion—not science as taught in schools, but science as experienced and debated. There was also a real appetite among scientists to explain their work and they too seemed to enjoy these evenings. Six months later, I looked on the Internet and discovered that some Cafés had started in France a year before, although with a different format. The idea was clearly a child of its time.

Things began to escalate. The Royal Society provided money to finance two series of Café evenings, one on science and science fiction, the other on science and society. The Wellcome Trust provided money to pay a part-time organizer to help spread the Cafés across the U.K., where there are now more than thirty, and the British Council took the idea worldwide, using the format in many different countries to seek out new audiences to discuss scientific ideas and issues. Meanwhile, people were picking up the idea off the Internet, and without any support (and usually without our knowledge!) Cafés began springing up in places like Brazil, Japan, Costa Rica, and even in such remote places as the U.S., where there are now about twenty. No one really knows how many regular Cafés there are—indeed I discovered a dozen while working on this piece.

Why are the Cafés so popular?

There are some obvious answers to this question. Science is moving up the public agenda as it directly affects our lives through medicine, nutrition, global warming, nuclear energy, genetically modified foods, and the like. Science stories now make headlines regularly in the news and on television; much of science is controversial and perhaps worrying, so that arouses interest and curiosity. But I think there is another reason. Through disciplines like genetics, neurology, pharmacology, and evolutionary psychology, science is giving us a new picture of what it means to be human. This is very different from the one we have received from literature, philosophy, religion, and much of the rest of our culture. Free will is at stake, sexual preference may be genetically determined, consciousness may be unzipped, and God is on trial. This fault line between the sciences and the rest of our culture directly affects us all and needs to be discussed and negotiated. This process will continue for as long as science addresses the basis of human nature and experience.

Those are theoretical reasons why the Cafés are popular, but there are practical ones as well. It is enjoyable to go out to a pleasant environment, which is also stimulating. Face-to-face interaction is rewarding, not just between scientists and the audience, but between members of the public, because the Cafés are usually friendly venues where it is easy to meet people, even if all you say to them is "I didn't understand a word of that—did you?" By chatting during the break, the audience gathers the confidence to ask questions they know others will also be interested in.

For the organizers, this is an easy and rewarding project. No money is required—speakers' expenses are paid by literally passing a hat around in the interval. There is no shortage of subjects—just read newspapers and magazines and new subjects crop up regularly. Local enterprise is the name of the game and formats can be as varied as you like. In France there are usually four speakers, in Denmark two—a scientist and an artist or someone from a related discipline. In Poland there are regular summer Cafés in a wooded campsite by a lake, in Glasgow in a shopping mall in the city centre, and in Rome on a riverboat. The subjects are as varied as the locations. In Brazil the first and very popular meeting was on the chemistry of beer, in Beijing on designer babies, in Moscow HIV in Russia, and in Leeds the future of alchemy. Meanwhile in Belgrade, they always make a cake to illustrate the topic under discussion. For a recent evolutionary biology evening they had an Australopithecus cake!

"Sometimes organizers worry about the quality of speakers, but that is not really an issue. It is the audience that makes the evening, rarely the speaker."

Sometimes organizers worry about the quality of speakers, but that is not really an issue. It is the audience that makes the evening, rarely the speaker. If the subject is interesting or controversial and the speaker is knowledgeable then the discussion will always be worthwhile. In many ways the speaker is only there to give the audience enough information to start asking intelligent questions; the evening develops from there.

Finally, for the organizers, it is a rewarding task. The number of people who say "thank you" afterwards or encourage you to continue creates a warm glow in your heart and you feel a saintly halo forming above your head.

What is the purpose of the Cafés?

Oliver Sacks, the writer and neurologist, said the point of the Cafés was to bring science back into culture. Some people see the point as increasing public understanding of science, some see it as science communication, some as science engagement or even science education. Undoubtedly the Café has elements of each of these, but I see the point as something rather different. If, as I believe, the liveliest part of the evening is the discussion and questions, then I think the Café is really a cultural examination of science. The audience is learning about one aspect of science and examining it from the outside, not the inside. This opens up a whole range of questions and issues that would not be covered by a debate within science itself.

"It is not a shop window for science, and the audience quickly picks up on that. There is no secret agenda to be entertaining but always supportive of science."

A great advantage of the Café Scientifique is that it is not a shop window for science, and the audience quickly picks up on that. There is no secret agenda to be entertaining but always supportive of science. One session could have a speaker in favour of nanotechnology and the next meeting could have someone dismissive of it. The members of the audience are left to make up their own minds, and this suits the period in which we live. Nineteenth-century scientific societies were vehicles for self-improvement. In the twenty-first century, people want to participate and develop their own views. The common thread of the Cafés is that science impinges on every culture, worldwide.

The science is pretty much the same, but the cultural responses are different, hence the different formats, topics, locations, etcetera. The overriding need is for culture to engage with the scientific ideas and draw science back into conversation.

There are consequences. If Cafés are a cultural investigation of science then they should be appropriate for any culture: high culture, popular culture, youth culture, ethnic culture, or whatever. This is what seems to be happening. A number of Cafés, in New York, London, and Copenhagen, to name just three, deal with the relationship between science and the arts, which you might call high culture. Popular culture is probably the area most Cafés deal in, where the subjects are of general interest or journalistic controversy.

Youth culture has been pioneered in France, which set up Junior Cafés in schools in 1999. The principles are that the students pick the topic and chair, and organize and advertise the event, which must not be held in a classroom, but can take place in the canteen, common room, or elsewhere. Speakers are usually chosen from a local university and any teacher is there just as an observer. As one teacher put it: "What surprised me was that the clever questions came not from the geeks, but from the long-haired Rastas in the room." Finding the right subjects and speakers can be a problem. One of the schools wanted the subject of the Café discussion to be dry cleaning—not an obvious academic discipline. However, the Junior Cafés have been successful in France and are now being copied in Britain and also in the U.S. Interestingly, in the U.S. they are taking place outside the school in a local café.

Ethnic culture is more difficult. In Britain we have recruited a Muslim woman to start a Café in a densely Muslim area of one city. The first meeting next month is on the subject of transplants, which is problematic for Islam—but the speaker is a Muslim transplant surgeon. We are doing the same with an Afro-Caribbean woman in another city in the north of England. We hope to find different formulae, in terms of subjects, speakers, and venues that will encourage discussion in these communities.

What of the future?

The Café Scientifique is bottom up, not top down. It is a voluntary network with no hierarchy, held together only by a central Web site and discussion list. Its growth and change are organic, not directed, so any projection into the future is personal rather than planned. However, we all have hopes, so let me spell them out.

Firstly, I hope the Cafés continue to grow here in North America and also in Europe and Japan, where there are already sixty. The U.S. has great potential for growth and the Cafés already here are lively, successful, and very innovative. In Europe, because of low-cost flights, we have the unusual situation that it is cheaper to get a speaker from Holland to Leeds than to bring one up from London, and if we can encourage cross-frontier speakers that would be a great benefit.

Secondly, I think the Muslim world is a great challenge. If we can find ways of encouraging the discussion of science in the Middle East in places like Iran, I think it would be a good thing and the Cafés might be one way to go about it. There are now Cafés in Isfahan, Karachi, and Ankara, and hopefully there will be further expansion.

Thirdly, the underdeveloped areas of the world present a peculiar challenge. In Africa there are now Cafés in Uganda, Kenya, and South Africa, with more to come in other countries. There the topics for discussion are very practical: HIV, malaria, water purification, TB, etcetera. In Uganda, Cafés are starting in local languages, often in "Malwa joints," where people prepare their local brew in a large pot and stand around drinking it through long straws. The informal nature of these Cafés provides a valuable tool for health education and the adaptation to local culture is a lesson for us all. In African schools the idea that science can be discussed, rather than just taught, is very popular with both teachers and pupils, and sometimes the Junior Cafés in Uganda have hundreds of pupils at a single session. So the Cafés may make science more accessible to both the young and old.

But meanwhile, I still enjoy our local sessions back home, and I look forward to our next meeting, where the subject is the psychological phenomenon of déjà vu. This is the first time we have treated this topic—I think.

How to Start a Science Café

Anyone can start a Science Café. Organizing one doesn't take an enormous effort or big budget. In fact, large, complicated, or high-profile events can take away from the casual, intimate café atmosphere. The scale of these events leads easily to an ongoing series, rather than a one-off event.

Understanding the basic concept

There are two shared values reflected in every Science Café:

- Science Cafés actively engage everyone attending.

- Science Cafés reach out to new audiences.

Steps to Organizing Your Own Science Café

- Connect with other organizers to see what others have done.

- Understand the audience you would like to attract.

- Give yourself a ten-week timeline from the initial planning meeting to event day.

- Create a budget. Some events cost virtually nothing. Most expenses are related to publicity, or travel for an out-of-town speaker.

- Choose a time and place. Go to where your audience congregates naturally. Unconventional venues seem to work best.

- Choose a moderator.

- Choose a Café topic. The best topics provoke a reaction in everyone.

- Choose a guest scientist.

- Prepare the guest scientist. He or she should offer a conversation starter, rather than a speech or lecture.

- Promote your Café. Word of mouth and email work best. Flyers in the café area can work. Find a partner organization to help out.

- Break the ice. There are a number of ways to get the conversation going after the guest presentation.

- Evaluate your Café.

C hristie Nicholson is freelance science journalist in New York. She hosts and produces the weekly audio podcast 60-Second Mind, and is an online contributor at Scientific American. For this book, Christie interviewed six leaders in the world of science about how the Web is affecting their communications practices.

Telling Science Stories on the Web: Interviews with Six Science Communicators on the Vanguard

Christie Nicholson

We are in the early days of the Web, a fact we often overlook. It was Christmas Day, two decades ago, when Tim Berners-Lee demonstrated the first Web server, browser, and page working together at CERN, a European particle-physics lab in Geneva. And already we have surpassed even the sort of online communication that was unimaginable a decade ago. Thanks to the exponential growth of ever-smaller and inexpensive computer chips, our media is experiencing a rate of change without precedent. And if we stop to think about it, our adaptation to this enormous change is remarkable. We grumble and moan when we can't get an immediate Wi-Fi signal or our video doesn't load, as if such things had always been with us. But as much as we've taken to the mouse as if it were an innate skill (ever watch a three-year-old work a mouse?), have we figured out how to maximize the medium for storytelling and, if we can still use this word, journalism? Many would argue we are nowhere close.

Even in the midst of trying to find a new foundation for journalism, the technology is ever changing and so makes for a constant challenge. I'd argue it's impossible to predict what impact digital technology will have on science journalism. But still it's fun to try. So I chatted with six science communicators to hear what amazes and disappoints them about the Web and their evolving profession. Their thoughts are intriguing, unusual, and hopeful.

I think the Web has so seamlessly woven itself into our lives because it satisfies an often forgotten human desire. We might not recognize it consciously, but humans have an inherent need to share information and experiences. Consider this: a child sees a kite flapping in the sky, and sure she's excited, but this is not what brings her ultimate satisfaction. No, that moment comes when she tugs on her mother's skirt, points up, and knows that her mother also sees the kite. This is the shared experience that humans crave and love.

"I think the Web has so seamlessly woven itself into our lives because it satisfies an often forgotten human desire. We might not recognize it consciously, but humans have an inherent need to share information and experiences."

It is this need for a shared experience that the primatologist Herbert Terrace says may have been the impetus for language. And I would argue it is this need for a shared experience that has fuelled the incredible popularity of all things related to online connectivity. Never before has a medium allowed multiple people to share with multiple people in real time.

There is one digital innovation that is central to this connectivity. The spectacle of the Web—applications like iTunes, Facebook, *World of Warcraft*—may be the most overt symbol of digital progress, but it is not the leap that fundamentally changed the way Web communication works. That innovation came decades before the Web existed—in 1968 it was known as "hypertext" or "hypermedia." It is now known as the "hyperlink" and it turns static text into something multi-dimensional. Linking words and phrases allows us to expand on or move deeper into any story. With links we can develop our own story, our own ending. We are in control, yet we also have the opportunity for serendipity. This is the infectious combo that is the crux of the Web.

The hyperlinks then bond all media, creating an entirely new format with audio, video, interactive graphics, and text layered together to tell a story. But no one has created a truly novel composition integrating all four media, yet. So far, we just paste the old media formats online. The *New York Times* site has loads of video, audio, and graphics but it still looks like a newspaper. Perhaps the new way to tell stories will come as a slow evolution, or a media sage will spark an original formula. We might recall that the classic inverted pyramid format of a news story—with the most important facts positioned at the top—developed during the Progressive Era. Research has shown that the modern news-story format came at a time when there was a surge in scientific discovery and a focus on facts as opposed to a narrative format. This question of how the Web might change modern storytelling is one of the questions six science communicators tackle in the following series of interviews about the Web, science, and stories.

John Rennie, the former editor-in-chief of *Scientific American*, recalls what reporting was like before the Web and predicts which eternal truths will permeate the current media shift. Clive Thompson, a freelance science writer, notes with no loss of enthusiasm that nothing spectacular has occurred yet on the Web. Greta and Dave Munger, the couple behind the popular blog *Cognitive Daily*, describe the joy of reigniting unscientific experiments on the Web. Robin Lloyd, an online editor at *Scientific American*, has such contagious passion for creativity on the Web that she is determined to find the online sweet spot for making science cool. And finally, Kristen Sanford, a scientist-turned-online-science-celebrity, says that it is the Web's hyper-connectivity that will be a boon for modern science knowledge.

Jonh Rennie is the former editor-in-chief at Scientific American, where he was on staff for twenty years. He is an award-winning journalist who has made radio and TV appearances too numerous to mention. As the founder of Scientific American's Observations, he is one of the earlier science bloggers I've known and is now, in his new position as a freelance science journalist, jumping deep into social media and the whole Web thing once again. After fifteen years as editor-in-chief of the world's pre-eminent science magazine, he is able to give a wider perspective on science communication, including a prediction of the eternal truths likely to survive the current upheaval in journalism.

CHRISTIE What has most surprised you on the Web?

JOHN   With the rise of the Web in general, one of the earlier questions might have been: Is there some sort of automated digital media that would be able to take the place of what journalists, reporters, and editors have been doing? And I might have answered: The great value the editors are bringing to all this is that they use a discriminating human intelligence to filter the quality information.

CHRISTIE You mean humans as the ultimate search engines?

JOHN   Go back to 1996 and look at the state of search engines like AltaVista and Yahoo!. It was easy to say they were useful in helping you get a lot of information, but you still needed the buffer of human intelligence to help make sense of it. A big part of what you did was comb through the results to get the most relevant stuff. What's been stupefying with the rise of Google and other sophisticated services is just how much high-level discrimination has been automated. At one time I would've been too quick to see this as a role editors would serve until we had a much more advanced state of artificial intelligence (AI) than we do. So without having that giant rise in AI, we have still found shortcuts.

CHRISTIE With respect to science journalism what is the best thing about digital media?

JOHN   How much it's possible for me, parked in my easy chair with a laptop, to find my way to endless amounts of information on any scientific topic. I never have to go to a library. As a freelancer I used to be really dependent on going to a public library.

CHRISTIE How often did you go to the library?

JOHN   Back in the days of yore I went once a week. I'd pull together the things I'd be working on a week ahead so I could get all the research done at once. These days you never have to go to a public library. That's sort of the bad side to this too. There's a library research skill that has disappeared.

CHRISTIE   But is that a useful skill?

JOHN   The issue is not one of valuable skill so much as there is so much online now that it can fool you into thinking everything is online. Everything isn't online. So the digital archives that are easily accessible are at a huge advantage, over the mountains of research that are still largely locked up on paper. It even puts at some disadvantage some things that are online but not as well connected. It privileges *Nature* and *Science* and the other big journals and puts at a disadvantage some of the smaller more specialized journals.

CHRISTIE   What else has the Web done to change your reporting and research?

JOHN   I think studying a network of blogs around a similar topic is good example. When I've been writing about, say, evolution or creationism, or things related to environmental topics—highly debated topics—there are certain blogs I go to, to find people who are passionate about these topics. For instance, it's easy for me to read something that P. Z. Myers writes as an angry reaction to something the intelligent-design people had written. For controversial topics, tapping into the blogs is a great way to research. It's not like going to a reference book and pulling out the facts. With the interconnectivity of communication on blogs you get a very clear sense of the hot-button points. And what counter-arguments work and don't work. And who are the voices that everyone listens to, and who seemingly gets ignored but seems to have a worthwhile point.

CHRISTIE   Accessing information on the Web is about speed. We're more and more addicted to the refresh button. How is speed affecting scientific communication?

JOHN   With science communication there are some kinds of explanation that you can only give by having sustained presentation. Say you're speaking to the average science-interested layperson and you need to get deep and gnarly on the subject of receptor proteins or histone chemistry. It's going to take you a while to lay the foundation. And because of that extra time, there may be a sieve reporters unconsciously apply, preferring stories that are easier to tell. It means going for the obvious stories with the punchlines. Lots of people like to read physics stories, and if we look at the kind of stories that make it into the general press there's a disproportionate amount on black holes, string theory, quantum weirdness stuff. If you generalize from those stories on how much of that constitutes what people actually work on in physics, you'd probably get a really distorted vision of the industry.

CHRISTIE   Will the Web change the traditional way we've told stories?

JOHN   I think there's no question people are finding new ways to tell stories and structure things. It really comes down to how big a space within the realm of science communication is going to be occupied by what we'd recognize as traditional commercial media outlets. If the future is one in which you still have plenty of commercial consumer media, the role of press releases and blog-like commentary will be more marginalized. If there isn't a business that will sustain traditional media, the other side of that will expand. Each of those three categories—traditional, press releases, and blogs—has its own form and style and its own language.

CHRISTIE   Can you briefly describe those?

JOHN   With commercial media, we have that pyramid-type structure. Press releases are designed to ape that structure, and hype it. When you get to the amateur blog level, amateur in the sense that they're doing it for the love, they are much less bound to the pyramid structure. With blogs you're in a situation where you have people who are communicating for an audience they assume knows something about what is going on. So it's more like listening in on an ongoing conversation. It may be more dominated by strong points of view, stronger language, by the winds and quirks of the different commenters, and those commenters may also be playing around with different forms.

CHRISTIE   So there may not be an inherent way of telling a story that will stick with us in the future?

JOHN   There are certain kinds of eternal verities. People like stories. People really, really like stories. Certain parts of that are the introduction, the rising arc of the body structure, and strong kicker conclusion. There's something very satisfying about that emotionally and intellectually. I do see that as a timeless human truth. It will be interesting to see in the future if media becomes inherently connected—whether people will see themselves as a giant network of other conversations that are going on, and whether or how much individual authors feel less and less obligation to provide a story

"There are certain kinds of eternal verities. People like stories. People really, really like stories."

structure. People may simply jump into the middle of the story and start shouting out points of view because the viewers can get all the rest of the back-story from someplace else.

CHRISTIE What about the experimentation with online video? When we see the myriad formats that have strayed so far from mainstream broadcast format, it appears storytelling via video could be blown wide open.

JOHN The great advantages of video for something like science stories is that there are some kinds of points you can make so quickly and elegantly with moving pictures.

CHRISTIE Can you give us an example?

JOHN George Musser's presentation in *Scientific American*'s video series *Instant Egghead*, about dark matter. It so tickled me because it helped me finally get the idea. He was able to say and show us: "All the stars of our galaxy should be spinning around at different speeds like crumbs in a coffee cup and they're not. They're spinning around in a fixed position as if they were on a compact disc." When you have those simple visuals of objects taken right off a desk—crumbs in coffee and a compact disc—you get a sense that dark matter is the unseen CD that holds this stuff in place. That's great. That really drives home easily and vividly a sense of what dark matter is.

CHRISTIE What is your dream digital future? Specific to science communication?

JOHN I'd love if there were somehow the tools that made it possible for me to show you what I'm thinking and make it as immediately accessible as possible. I'd love to be able to produce Pixar-quality animation, based on simple stickmen figures and word descriptions that can be found in an archive. For me to assemble an animation just based on research, in the same way there are free online tools now—that would be really cool and they would always be there for me as tools of a journalist. With the rise of digital media there is more of an equalizer in effect than ever before. It's a matter of expanding the tool kit available to everybody.

Dave and Greta Munger are the couple behind what was one of the most popular psychology blogs online, Cognitive Daily. Greta is a professor of psychology at Davidson College, North Carolina, and Dave is a freelance science writer and editor of ResearchBlogging.org. They started Cognitive Daily five years ago* with the intention of writing a book. But what was supposed to be a repository for interesting book content wound up being a limitless final product that drew thousands of readers. The Mungers take unusual advantage of one of the unique qualities of the Web: interactivity. Their most popular posts were "Casual Fridays," in which they posted weekly surveys or quizzes. The resulting patterns, from audience answers, helped illustrate larger scientific principles.

*While Cognitive Daily closed shop on January 20, 2010, the archives still live on here: http://scienceblogs.com/cognitivedaily/.

CHRISTIE On your blog *Cognitive Daily*, you covered a lot of research that falls outside of the press-release cycle. That's refreshing.

GRETA Yes, I would get curious about something and then use PsycINFO or PubNet to find an article. So we didn't often write about something that was just published, but the science was still good. I don't like the idea that, in science, if you publish it today it's good but if you publish it yesterday it's no good.

CHRISTIE So you think that's a misconception about scientific study?

GRETA Part of the problem is that people don't really understand how science works and the fact that you do your experiment and it takes time. I mean, it could take five years to collect the data and when you finally publish it's not like you're done—it's a longer process. Old data can be current. Current science lasts a long time.

CHRISTIE But the Web has made speed and immediacy paramount. The Web doesn't have time for yesterday's info.

DAVE In some ways the Web is a little constricting because people are expecting to see very recent stuff. On the other hand, what the Web allows you to do that you can't do in other media are things like include a video or survey. We did a lot of interactive stuff with our readers. It worked really well for us because we'd come up with a quick survey that demonstrated the principle that the research is talking about. So even if people are skeptical about the research they could do our survey and see the pattern of the survey results, then maybe say, okay it is true.

CHRISTIE So you started *Cognitive Daily* with the intention of eventually turning it into a book. It's been five years and no book. Why?

GRETA We decided we really don't want to do a book, because it's really limiting, especially in terms of the lack of interactivity and the demands that publishers put on you. They want this narrative that is distinct and usually science doesn't work that way. We found we were better able to get our message across in the blogging format.

CHRISTIE Can you unpack that?

GRETA I don't have a grand scientific theory I'm promoting. I like seeing the little pieces and trying to understand the moments of the way people are interacting with their world.

DAVE And that doesn't lend itself to a book. The online world allows people to approach issues and problems in different ways.

CHRISTIE Will the Web allow for new ways to tell a story?

GRETA I think people look for patterns. So we tell ourselves stories. We create a narrative, a story in our heads about what's going on throughout our days. I'd say storytelling is fundamental to the way we process information. The amount of information that is getting into the mind is very little compared to how rich our experience of the world is. With vision you can look at a fuzzy blur which is actually the light hitting our retina. But you never see a fuzzy blur, you see a world because we're threading together our experience. Part of that is storytelling.

CHRISTIE And what about the stories we get from the Web versus traditional print stories?

DAVE The interesting thing is that there is a larger story that the blog reader creates, because they are with that blogger day in and day out. In a newspaper, usually a reporter is faceless. In a blog, people get to you know you, there are characters, because we talk about kids, about each other, how we feel, little anecdotes about our lives. That's all woven into these stories about science.

CHRISTIE You conducted surveys on your blog where you engaged readers to participate and see the results. I still find them fascinating and surprisingly engaging. Tell us more about them.

DAVE   With "Casual Fridays" [the weekly survey or quiz posted to their blog that explores a possible real-life pattern or experimental principle] it's getting people to think about experimental design. The first Casual Friday survey was based on an observation from when I go running. It seemed like other runners said "hi" to me, but no one else did. So to see if this is a general principle, we asked people who they said "hi" to when they are out and who said "hi" to them. Sure enough dog walkers say "hi" to other dog walkers. And it works that way for every single example. What's great from my perspective is that our readers pointed out that our surveys aren't really scientific. And that's true, but the fact that they're saying that, they're still learning something about science.

CHRISTIE   This sort of interactivity is a key change with the Web. Has it surprised you to see the extent to which people are willing to interact?

GRETA   We had no idea *Cognitive Daily* would be popular. We didn't do anything to announce it; we just did it for this book that never happened. One thing we did that I really liked is that we'd give people the details of the method so you can begin to understand why the researcher can say what they're saying. That's important to me. This nitty-gritty aspect gets ignored with mainstream reporting.

CHRISTIE   What is the best thing that digital media has done for science communication?

DAVE   It's made science more approachable. People are realizing that scientists are real people and they can talk to them. Real scientists are providing information on blogs and you can follow a scientist on Twitter and they'll talk about what they're doing in their labs.

CHRISTIE   What's the worst thing?

DAVE   It's so easy to put up pseudo-science, anybody with $15 can set up a Web site now and make it look authoritative.

CHRISTIE   Is there any way to curb that?

DAVE   I do think a site like ResearchBlogging.org, where only peer-reviewed research is posted, helps. Obviously we're not offering a guarantee on that site that everything is 100 percent accurate and true, but at least it gives you confidence that there has been some vetting going on. The fact that the Web is interactive—you can use your Twitter feed so that if you see something you're skeptical of you can ask scientists about it—there's more of a way to verify if this thing is real or not.

CHRISTIE What are some of the quirky, more creative pieces you remember from the Web?

GRETA Michael Bock presents classic visual illusions online with explanations. You can immediately get the illusion and it's beautifully done.

CHRISTIE When did you come across that?

GRETA Five years ago. I was working on a lecture and typically I search online to find something I can use to illustrate whatever I'm teaching. He had exactly what I was looking for. It's been around for quite awhile … there's this thing called point light displays, they used to do it where you actually attach little light bulbs to the joints of someone and then film them in the dark so you have an animation of where their joints were as they walk. Now you can do it on the computer. You can adjust how masculine or feminine the walk is, or how happy or sad the walker is. You can see right away how much information we get from this very minimal stimulus. It's much easier to explain the effect with a picture.

CHRISTIE Has the Web changed the way you teach?

GRETA Yes. Before the Web I'd have had this static image xeroxed from a journal article on an overhead. Or I might have read off a bunch of words describing the experiment. But having the Web and a computer projector has allowed me to do more demonstrations and it really helps students understand what I'm talking about.

CHRISTIE If you could be in charge, where would you want digital information to go?

DAVE I want to see a lot more scientists talking about research and their areas online in a lot of different forms. Some might be on Facebook, blogs, Twitter, YouTube, whatever way they feel is a good way of sharing what they do with the public. Right now, probably less than one percent of scientists are sharing their work in this way.

GRETA Part of the problem with Dave's vision is that the way you write your papers for the other scientists and the way you write on *Cognitive Daily* are very different skill sets. *Cognitive Daily* worked because Dave is a really good science writer.

CHRISTIE This is a point that keeps coming up in any discussion about Web communication. Can amateur communicators take over?

DAVE It's not necessarily the case that everybody has to be a good communicator. I think there are some scientists who are good communicators. I guess in my dream world this would work. Those people might do a little more to evangelize not just their own but others in their field. The way Michael Bock does optical illusions and shares others on his site. It's not just about doing public relations for your own lab but sharing the type of work you do with the world.

CHRISTIE Greta, if you were in charge, where would you want digital information to go?

GRETA I'm so bad at these future things. I'm just going to see what happens and play with it.

Robin Lloyd has been an old-school beat science reporter since the early '90s and was a senior editor at LiveScience.com and SPACE.com. She's now the news editor, online, at Scientific American. She has a new-found passion for creating interesting stories on the Web and plans to use the Internet to ignite her master plan to make science more engaging than it's ever been. She loves her tiny Flip video camera and, unlike most traditional journalists, cannot wait to see what the next big digital shift might be.

CHRISTIE What was the first thing that amazed you about the Web—within the realm of science?

ROBIN I don't want to speak in clichés, but it was the interactivity and Flash animation. I wasn't seeing a lot of stuff that blew me away until the work of Anatoly Zak. He was a Russian immigrant I worked with and he knew a lot about Russian spacecraft. He was also a graphic artist and created a Flash animation of the International Space Station. The density of clickable information blew me away. On a static print page, you're limited. On the Web, there's no limit.

CHRISTIE   What are the most remarkable differences between the Web and traditional print?

ROBIN   Kids say, "I don't need to find the news, the news finds me." There are so many ways that the news comes to us now. I mean, Twitter is the number-one vehicle for me. Yahoo! recently launched its new home page. They've got all these little modules and I can just roll over what's going on at Time Inc., what's going on at NPR, what's going on at *Boing Boing*. I don't have to go to the Web sites to see what's going on. I've got RSS [Real Simple Syndication, which means syndicated online feeds of published information] and I just go to my RSS reader. The Web is so huge now with the number of pages and sites and opportunities.

CHRISTIE   How has the Web helped you as a science reporter?

ROBIN   I started out in newspapers in the 1990s and there's no comparison. It was difficult to write about science before the Web. If I was writing about HIV or astrophysics, the only research I had was stuff I pulled from clip files. I could ask my sources or pull a book off the shelf, but you only have so many books and time. I was filing two or three stories a day. A science story is no good if it's not dense. You need to contextualize it. A science story didn't just happen within an hour, or a week, or over months—it's been happening since the dawn of knowledge! It helps if you can capture some of that huge time frame, and the Web allows for that.

"A science story didn't just happen within an hour, or a week, or over months—it's been happening since the dawn of knowledge! It helps if you can capture some of that huge time frame, and the Web allows for that."

CHRISTIE Are you creating more material now?

ROBIN   There's a human limit. I don't think I'm much more productive now than I was then, in terms of quantity. But the Web allows me to tell much higher-quality stories. When I was at a wire service I had days that I filed fourteen stories. I was prolific, but the material was shallow. Now you can put in more background. And you can feel more confident about the facts. Now everyone of us (reporter, editor, and copy editor) can fact check at every level of the editing phase. There's a higher accuracy with science journalism now.

CHRISTIE Do you think the structure of storytelling will change with the Web?

ROBIN   There is something basic about story structure that is going to endure, but there's no question that the Web modifies that basic structure and we will continue to modify it. Many of us are focused now on search engine optimization, where we structure our stories in such a way so that we generate more traffic. And because of this, one of the things that is falling away is the anecdotal lead.

CHRISTIE Why?

ROBIN   There aren't a lot of searchable words at the top of the story with an anecdotal lead. So search engines aren't as likely to pull up a story with an anecdotal lead as relevant to someone who is searching for a specific topic. So with long-form journalism on the Web, for example, that isn't the greatest match.

CHRISTIE So what is the most positive change that could happen to stories on the Web?

ROBIN   Proliferation. There are more avenues now, more verticals, as they say, for getting your science information. There's just more contact with science than there used to be. Science information and science journalists are more accessible. I think there was less of a premium on that fifteen years ago and now I feel like accessibility is king.

CHRISTIE You love your tiny Flip video camera. Why?

ROBIN   The news cycle has contracted with the Web. So deadlines are rolling. The Flip cuts down production time, and what we're learning with YouTube is that consumers do not demand high-quality video. Sometimes a very raw piece of video is more compelling than something that is well produced, because there is this feeling of authenticity. I can shoot something happening right in front of our offices in Manhattan and upload it to YouTube and then Tweet it. I can break stories in a minute. That being said, the tools are so easy that the Web has forced a breakdown of the division between who's a journalist and who's not.

CHRISTIE So if there is a breakdown in that division, what's going to distinguish quality?

ROBIN   I think it's trust. I think it's about generating trust between the consumer and producer. I'm not using the word "journalist" nor am I using the word "reader."

There are people who generate it and people who consume it, and many are both at this point. Right now, though, I think the journalist is the person we trust to do the job right.

CHRISTIE   But what ultimately brings trust?

ROBIN   Reliability and accuracy are basic standards for journalism, and they're standards for all of our human interactions. I think that over time people who consume news learn to recognize information that is accurate and reliable. I think consumers know the difference between a blog and an item that is written or produced by staff at a Web site. They know that material on a blog is not as trustworthy as material on certain Web sites.

CHRISTIE   What is one of the more useful science news pieces you've seen on the Web?

ROBIN   The *New York Times* did something when swine flu broke. They had this neat map showing where the clusters of cases were coming up over time. It was reassuring at a time when things were very uncertain. There was something about that interactive map that told me what was going on. I had been on that beat for a week. I really knew what was going on. I had already read thousands of words on the topic and yet when I saw the graph, I could immediately see it was really affecting only New York City and Mexico. So I saw the big picture for the H1N1 outbreak with more clarity, which allowed me to pull back from covering it as a daily breaking story and shift more into "monitor and keep an eye out for" features mode.

CHRISTIE   What do you want to do with digital journalism? Where do you want it to go?

ROBIN   Cheap video. The market will demand that everybody works for less and we'll need to generate this stuff more efficiently. Five years from now I want more concise video that shows how science is done. What the scientific method is and why it's important. Humanitarian efforts depend on reason and empirical knowledge, knowledge that is generated via the scientific method. That link has been eroded in the last thirty-five years.

CHRISTIE   Why has it eroded?

ROBIN   A lot of people think: I don't know about this science thing, but when I come down with swine flu I sure hope there's a vaccine for me. Well, guess what? The vaccine for swine flu is generated as a result of people using the scientific method.

They went on scientific facts that were a result of collecting data and analyzing it in a rational way. Often people don't get that connection; they think it's magic. I'm not sure why the connection to the scientific method eroded, but I imagine it has to do with the trend in the U.S. toward valuing materialism and consumption more highly than excellence and courage.

CHRISTIE So how can the Web engage people in the scientific method?

ROBIN   We hook them with the cool. How vaccines are made can be just as cool as Britney Spears. In fact, she gets boring pretty fast and we're on to the next thing. But developments in science are a freaking riot, if you tell the story in a way that conveys how cool the people involved are, how cool the findings are, and how relevant they are. The Web makes it easier to tell stories, gives us more ways to tell stories, and we can get the stories to people more quickly. There's this immediacy, and with this immediacy we convey authenticity to people. Thereby we can strengthen our relationship with consumers of our news, users, visitors, and promote this grand plan that I have.

CHRISTIE And what is this grand plan?

ROBIN   My grand plan is that I want to make science news more accessible, easier to create, more relevant, and more engaging by bringing to bear the interactivity, immediacy, and excitement that online multimedia and non-press-release-generated journalism provides, in order to promote justice, courage, reason, rationality, and excellence in society.

C*live Thompson is a science and technology writer in New York. He is a contributor to Wired, the New York Times, Fast Company, and other publications. He has written some of the more insightful pieces out there about the Web, Twitter, and video games. Clive is Canadian and a musician. On a regular day Clive speaks incredibly fast, but when you get him on a Skype call for an interview about science communication on the Web, he slides into highest gear.*

CHRISTIE What is the most innovative thing you've seen on the Web?

CLIVE   I don't think people have done anything very innovative at all with communication online. This is partly because of the type of thing that Marshall McLuhan talks about when he talks about the evolution of media.

CHRISTIE Can you expand on that? (Ten points for bringing up a Canadian.)

CLIVE   He pointed out that every time we get a new medium, we don't know what to do with it yet, so all we do is fill it with content in the same format as the last medium. So the first time people started doing radio they were just reading written text. They didn't realize that radio rewards a different type of communication—conversations between two people. Or recording something live and bringing it to listeners—time shifting an event. When TV came along they made the same mistake. They basically said okay, this is TV. Hmm, so TV is like radio with pictures, right? Eventually with TV they realized we can illustrate things that are hard to describe in text. But that gain took ten years or longer to figure out. So as far as I'm concerned I don't think people have figured out what is generically new about communicating on the Web. Because, yeah, you can put video online, but who cares? It's just video, same as it was before. You can put audio up, same as before. You can put text up; it's just text.

CHRISTIE But if you had to say where the innovation is on the Web, what would you say?

CLIVE   Where you see new forms of communication coming along. The thing that illustrates what the medium is good at doing is the sort of dense writing you sometimes see on blogs.

CHRISTIE Meaning what?

CLIVE   Blogs, especially science blogs, where they understand that the ability to hyperlink online that allows for a type of density of expression. Because your audience can follow a link through to what you are writing about. And this allows for two useful meanings: one is the actual sentence as it's written, the other one is the meaning of the sentence after you've gone and looked at what the link is pointing to. The science writer Steven Johnson first identified this in his book *Interface Culture* in 1999. He looked at Suck.com, which was this wry, sardonic, pop-culture blog, and he pointed out that people couldn't understand the sentences. And that's because the sentences didn't make any sense unless you followed all the hyperlinks—there were fourteen links in a 120-word paragraph. Obviously they were doing it playfully. But the point remains that the hyperlink is the most intellectually revolutionary thing about online text. People use it without thinking enough about how powerful that cognitive technique is. That's one thing that excites me.

CHRISTIE What else?

CLIVE   The fact that now as a science journalist you can have an ongoing relationship with your readership.

CHRISTIE   And what you mean by "ongoing" is that you keep the relationship open as you are reporting?

CLIVE   Right. Whether you're blogging or Twittering or communicating with people on Facebook, you can break up your thinking into thoughts and bits of reportage as you go along. The previous way of doing journalism was you collect for a long time in private and then you release this big thing.

CHRISTIE   Who is doing this well right now?

CLIVE   The great science journalist Carl Zimmer is always blogging about what he's thinking about as he's researching. So you get a bunch of interesting thoughts and you see him thinking through a subject and you see the piece when it comes out. I find it quite pleasant because you watch his intellect drifting toward the subject matter, wrestling with it, and then you see the final product when it comes out.

CHRISTIE   And the conversation with readers can prove helpful in terms of actual research, right?

CLIVE   If I'm working on something and get stuck on a question, I'll mention it on Twitter: "Does anyone know X, Y, Z?" I have thousands of followers so I can find stuff out really quickly. I could probably save myself a lot of work by aggressively working with my smart, core fans and exploring stories that way.

CHRISTIE   What is the most remarkable difference between the Web and, say, a book?

CLIVE   The Internet is an experience. You dip into it several times a day, emailing, looking at the news, dipping into a discussion, replying, and so you can't just say, "This isn't as good as a book." It's not trying to be a book. Twitter and Facebook critics say the same thing, "Why would I just want to sit down and see a bunch of tiny stupid little meaningless updates from people?" And it's true; you look at the individual updates, it says, "look at this site," or "I feel this way," or "I thought of this." But if you follow someone for three months you get an unbelievably rich sense of what that person is like. You get an amazing exposure to them. Social scientists call it ambient awareness. These epiphanies are going to become part of how journalism works.

CHRISTIE Where does this leave long-form stories? Books?

CLIVE For sheer immersion and depth of understanding it's tough to beat a book. I think print-on-demand technology is poised to blow open book publishing. It will reduce the costs of the endeavour to almost nothing and put all the profits in the hands of the author. Journalism is about getting people to pay attention to things, and what modern communications technology does is give people new ways to pay attention to things.

CHRISTIE What about online video?

CLIVE I'm very skeptical about video as a way to communicate information. I've seen myself doing the same discussion of a story in print, then on radio, then on TV. People who read my print story had a complete grasp of what they read. If they heard me on the radio they tend to have some memory of what was said. But if they see me on TV, they'll remember seeing me but won't remember a thing I said.

CHRISTIE Some of the fastest-growing subcultures in online video have to do with explanatory video or what I call the "visual encyclopedia."

CLIVE There are some fascinating studies that have argued that science is retained when students have direct interaction with a science teacher explaining things in the classroom. So if you need a person explaining stuff to you, maybe some awesome explanatory video is a really amazing thing for getting science out to younger people. I think we don't have a damn clue because we're just beginning to experiment with new forms.

CHRISTIE Do you think the traditional printed form, the inverted pyramid, for instance, will be replaced by new forms of storytelling?

CLIVE It's a great question if the inverted pyramid is destined for future use. There's something about that format that is inherently cognizant with the way our brains are optimized to understand information. I think some part of it will be pre-served moving forward. It's interesting how the literary forms get re-sampled in new media in cool ways. I was a headline writer at the *Globe and Mail*. And with headline writing you have to take a story's meaning and truncate it. When Twitter came along, everyone had to say something complex in 140 characters. The way people construct Tweets reminds me of headline writing. It's interesting to watch people stumble upon the same techniques that headline writers have been using for decades.

CHRISTIE On that point of shortened text, do you think brevity on the Web is killing the much-needed context in science stories?

CLIVE I had a debate with a woman about whether science journalism is incompatible with Tweeting. She felt that Tweeting could never give the context that a science journalist is ethically bound to provide. I told her it begs the question: What is too short? If 140 characters is too short, is three hundred words too short? Is two hundred too short? I've written seven-thousand-word stories for the *New York Times* and left out most of what I wanted to say!

If you, as a science journalist, are confident that a study was done well and you've read comments by other scientists that support this, then I don't have any problem with assuming I've an intelligent readership and giving them a three-word summary link to it. Would you rather have a story that's read by no one? Or a mechanism to push it out to people who can read it even if they don't have a science journalist at their shoulder helping to interpret it?

CHRISTIE What is the future for newspapers?

CLIVE Newspapers are screwed because print news has become a commodity. People want to know what just happened in Russia, or what happened with Michael Jackson's doctor. They want to know what just happened with that tremor in San Francisco. They don't care where the news comes from. If it came form the Associated Press that's fine, if it came from *Pravda*, that's fine … newspapers are screwed because it's a commodity like water. People want clean water and don't care where the water comes from.

CHRISTIE And other media?

CLIVE Other media don't necessarily have that problem. Nobody gets up in the morning and says, "I want to read a magazine today." If they do say that and you hand them *Cosmopolitan* they say, "Oh, I was thinking of *Scientific American*." Magazines have extremely strong brands. They are a luxury product and luxury products tend to find a way to survive.

CHRISTIE But the entire industry is changing mainly because the cost of producing any content is dropping

"I had a debate with a woman about whether science journalism is incompatible with Tweeting. She felt that Tweeting could never give the context that a science journalist is ethically bound to provide. I told her it begs the question: What is too short?"

to nearly zero. How are journalists going to survive when anyone can jump in? Should science journalists survive?

CLIVE   I've been an amateur musician my whole life. I'm forty years old, I've been playing guitar for twenty-four years. About seven years ago two things happened: home-recording software became really good and I can now use the Internet to distribute what I record. I have four mics that cost $400. If I'd bought them ten years ago they would've cost me $5,000. I don't need to make money at this; it's just my pastime, but I can produce stuff that is 80 percent of the quality I hear on the radio. So I encounter musician friends who are pissed off that their business model is falling apart, and I'm on the other side. Journalists are also on the flip side of a similar coin. Journalism has become unbelievably cheap to do and easy to distribute. It's encouraged a whole bunch of people who don't need to make any money on it, but can do stuff that is 80 percent as good. People are beginning to commit acts of journalism, acts of informing the public, acts of directing the public's attention, that are nearly as good as when I get paid a lot of money for it, and I spend six months at it.

CHRISTIE   So it's a good thing to welcome amateurs to the game?

CLIVE   In some ways because science journalism has been a be-knighted thing, because it's been drummed out of regular media—I almost think that we'd be better off if we say, let's just have amateurs do it and have really good scientists communicate with the public, because it can't possibly be worse than the average science stories in newspapers. Meanwhile, you have universities curating and packaging videos and descriptions of what their professors are doing. Some of it is self-serving but I've rarely seen them flat out lie about stuff. I want to continue making a living at this and I'm better than most amateurs at this, but not all. Obviously, as a professional, the value I bring is discovering good stories and explanations, and bringing them to an audience. But there's no reason amateurs couldn't do this too. The Internet does a really good job curating and bringing all the science information that often gets left out in mainstream media to people through blogs and Twitter posts. I don't regard that as competition for what I do; I think it's really cool stuff.

Kristen Sanford, a.k.a. Dr. Kiki, is a neurophysiologist who loves making science look cool. In fact, she loves inspiring others with science so much that she left the lab to make it her life goal. Ten years ago she created the podcast "This Week in Science," which reaches tens of thousands of listeners. She appears in a number of Web video series, and keeps a regular blog and an action-packed Twitter feed. She believes the Web offers a huge opportunity to get science into places it's never been.

CHRISTIE What is the first thing that struck you about the Web?

KRISTEN The change from just Web sites to creating communities. For my own radio show, the development of the online audio format mp3 was huge. We built a Web site in 2001 and we put up these mp3 files and all of a sudden it was like, oh my gosh, wow, one hundred people downloaded the show. And it was this step-by-step progression from the mp3s to the RSS feed which allowed people to subscribe. From there iTunes was really a huge benefit to getting these new media formats out to the public. I think that the increase in online communities in 2005 was gigantic. It gave everybody in the new-media industry a huge boost.

CHRISTIE What online communities strike you as really innovative?

KRISTEN Ning.com, started by Gina Bianchini, which allows people to design an online community for anything. It's sites like Ning that have made community building something anybody can do. There's been a lot of community building since Friendster started things off in 2002. Here on the west coast there was Tribe, then MySpace, and then Facebook. They've all just kind of built on top of each other and now Twitter is pretty big. But the next step has to involve interlinking a lot more information. But we'll need a huge database-type project to be able to do it.

CHRISTIE One of the big changes with the Web is that those who were consumers of science media can now be producers. Do you see any issues with this new distribution of knowledge?

KRISTEN The downside is that you're not assured of credibility. In science you can get a lot of people walking that fine line between pseudo-science and real science. There's nobody there to peer review it, and say, "Look, they haven't conformed to the standards of the scientific method." If you don't have a team look at the information from the community and deem it accurate and credible, then you have a real problem with things getting passed around that aren't real and can hurt the public's understanding of science.

CHRISTIE What about reputation growing over time? Or can the community self-police?

KRISTEN Yes, a lot of people are recently talking about "people ranking" on the Web. Instead of page rank there's this idea of people rank. Your reputation could possibly go with you from site to site to site. When you post on other people's blogs, or with any article that you publish anywhere on the Web, you are linked to all those things via your reputation. So you become known as credible or not, as a purveyor of information.

CHRISTIE Are there any advantages of having consumers as producers of scientific knowledge?

KRISTEN By allowing people to dabble in creating scientific information you increase the number of voices involved in the conversation about science. And by doing that you increase the ability of science to get out to more people. All these people who start dabbling have their own friends and their own communities and once they start putting stuff out there, they're like, "Hey, I did this thing, and you should listen to this show." They want to tell people about it; it increases the visibility, and by opening it up it really makes science appear to be what it really is, which is an ongoing open conversation about how the universe works.

CHRISTIE Do you think the Web is going to be a boon for science?

KRISTEN I think that only within the last couple of years has the public's interest in science, the communication of science, and citizen science, blown up in a big way. People want to get involved. There's a momentum to it that is just going to keep moving forward.

CHRISTIE Define "citizen science."

KRISTEN Citizen science is people who are not scientists in a laboratory, but who are still doing science in the real world. For example, scientists are using bird watchers. They're using people who are just bird watchers, but those bird watchers go out on a specific day and record whatever bird species they see in a particular location. That data can be used to help scientists understand how birds are moving through the environment and what is happening to that population. There are many different applications of what citizen science is, but the fundamental core is that it is taking science out of the laboratory and turning everyone into a scientist.

CHRISTIE   Will the Web fundamentally change the way we tell stories?

KRISTEN   What needs to happen that hasn't happened yet is the creation of layered media content. For instance, you have a story that you're reading and as you're reading it you mouse over a word or phrase, and that starts an audio file which gives you an idea of how things sound. Or a video file can open up. There's all sorts of ways that media can be creatively interspersed into text to make it part of the story. People aren't doing this yet because it takes that extra time and work. Especially when all you've been doing up to now is typing up your story, your editor okays it, and you put it out. It takes a lot more foresight to think about how I can supplement the story visually and aurally.

CHRISTIE   Who is doing the best integration of all media online right now?

KRISTEN   The people who are hitting the nail on the head in terms of creating content and making it interesting and being creative is *The Quest* on the west coast. It's a PBS program out of KQED. They've got real community involvement and they're really building something that is just awesome. I think they're at the top of creativity for communication in the multimedia realm.

CHRISTIE   What specifically are they doing?

KRISTEN   They've reached out into the public realm in a way that has drawn people to them. They've done a really good job of creating online video stories that complement their television programs. They have discussions where people have input into future stories. They have educational content that supplements teachers' curricula. They've got blogs. They've created as many ways as possible to interact with the information. They've got photos, they've got audio, they've got video. And you can embed their video and share it. It's not just stuck within their Web site.

CHRISTIE   What is your dream digital gadget?

KRISTEN   I want a neural uplink into everyone's brain. My voice in their head: "Science, science!"

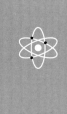

Great Tweets of Science

 newton chillin' in my garden, listening to- oww!!!
12:17 PM Oct 1666 from WoolsTwit.com

 newton had apple for lunch.
12:18 PM Oct 1666 from WoolsTwit.com

 Aristotle RT @Plato @Socrates "be as you wish to tweet"
8:50 AM 343 BC from AlexanTwit.com in reply to alex_da_great

 watson @crick It's a double helix! sck it, @pauling !!!!!
5:15 PM Feb 28th 1953 from TweaglePub.com

 chris_columbuz land ahead. anyone know a good Indian restaurant?
2:02 AM Oct 12th from santamariadeck.com

 albert-e OH at the grocery store: "ever notice how the line to pay moves slower when you're in a hurry?" [hmmm...]
2:036 PM Sep 27th 1905 from mobile

 nasa #followeveryday @armstrong @collins @aldrin
8:17 PM Jul 20th from HousTwit.com in reply to sputnik

 darwin1 I'm on a boat! I'm on a boat! check out thz crazy turtles, yoooo http://twitpic.com/abfze
4:09 PM Sep 15th 1835 from TheTweagle.com in reply to GOD

www.phdcomics.com

I t is widely believed that class size is an obstacle to successful science teaching, but maybe it is not always a
question of scale. Presented here are a yin-yang combination of science teaching initiatives that step outside the
scale issue. The first is *Iron Science Teacher*, a celebration
of teaching that reaches an audience of several thousand
each year. It is counterbalanced by "The Ultimate Lesson
Plan," by Leslie Reid, which explores what teaching is really
all about—an audience of one (the learner). Leslie Reid holds
the Tamaratt Teaching Professorship in Geoscience at the
University of Calgary in Alberta, Canada.

Iron Science Teacher

Mary Anne Moser

Think of a science teacher who inspired you. If you can't, it's remarkable that you even picked up this book. Teachers can have an enormous influence as students are stepping toward their science-related careers.

Iron Science Teacher is a celebration of one of the most important challenges in teaching—the ability to engage students fully. It is a contest, a nationwide search for Canada's best science teachers, focusing on teachers' ability to engage and entertain. As Nobel laureate Herbert Simon said, "Teaching is not entertainment, but it is unlikely to be successful unless it is entertaining."[1]

In Canada, the program started in Alberta in 2006, and was expanded in 2007 to involve partners across the country. The event follows a format similar to the famous *Iron Chef* television series, with teachers entering regional competitions to earn a place in the national finals. The regional events take place at science centres—one in the Atlantic provinces, one in Ontario and Quebec, a third in the Prairie provinces, and the last two in Alberta and British Columbia. The teachers are given a "secret ingredient" around which they have to present an engaging and imaginative lesson in science. The ingredient can be anything—the first year it was colour, the next year the body. We have used candy and water bottles. At the San Francisco Exploratorium, where they have been holding Iron Science Teacher events for over a decade, they use ingredients like fruitcake and marshmallows. The ingredient is not really a secret, because the teachers need to prepare their ten-minute sketches in advance. They tend to pull out all the stops, using fire, music, choreography, and drama.

The winners of the five regional playoffs are sent to compete in the Iron Science Teacher finals at the University of Calgary. Discovery Channel is the media partner, so the event is promoted on television, and the final contest is Webcast by Discovery Channel, watched live in classrooms around the country.

Iron Science Teacher is an example of science communication projects that can have considerable impact by scaling up. To make projects work at this level, we have learned some important lessons.

1. You don't have to have a good idea, you just need to recognize one. The Iron Science Teacher concept originated at the Exploratorium in San Francisco in

1995, where it involves Bay Area teachers and continues to yield a rich online set of Iron Science Teacher Webcasts. With the Exploratorium's blessing and advice, we turned it into a nationwide contest in Canada.

2. Partnerships are key. We can accomplish much more by collaborating than we can on our own. Iron Science Teacher in Canada involves science centres and museums, media partnerships, science outreach organizations, and critical sponsors.

3. Start with the audience. We know that everyday science teaching is not a contest, nor a spectacle. However, we wanted to draw attention to the importance of great science teachers. One way to do this was to stage an event that would attract an audience and have one main message—great science teaching makes science engaging. Our concept had to be exciting; in the world of television and the Internet, if you bore your audience, you don't have an audience. We were not really thinking about how to translate science concepts to a large audience, but we were focused on getting a larger audience to appreciate science and science teaching.

4. Science itself is fascinating. There is no need to be afraid of science content, or to candy coat it. Science actually contains more fascinating ideas than you could make up. But it seems to have an image problem. Science is often presented as good for you rather interesting in its own right, even though it helps people make sense of the world around them.

The photo feature here shows the tension, drama, spectacle, and excitement created by the Iron Science Teacher program.

1 David Pratt, *The Impossible Takes Longer: The 1,000 Wisest Things Ever Said by Nobel Prize Laureates* (Vancouver: Douglas and McIntyre, 2007), 91.

THIS PAGE Pre-show set-up at the 2007 Iron Science event. Photo Darren Colton

THIS PAGE Backstage with the Manitoba team in 2008: April McKnight, Adrian Deakin, Anil Sharma, and Cam Grier. Photo Ewan Nicholson

OPPOSITE Five hundred Grade 8 students in the audience. Photo Darren Colton

THIS PAGE The Enzymatics in 2007: Don Lacy, Jim Milross, Glen Fatkin, Briar Ballou. Photo Darren Colton

OPPOSITE Isabel Valoria, a Schulich School of Engineering student who led the crowd in a half-time dance break. Photo Ewan Nicholson

THIS PAGE Winners announced in 2007: Max Hegel, Grant Shaw, Kevin Zuk, and Carolina Nario, with hosts Jay Ingram and Nicole Stamp on the right. Photo Darren Colton

The Ultimate Science Lesson Plan

Leslie Reid

Step 1: Strip your lesson down to the big idea

When creating the ultimate science lesson plan, start with a sharp focus on the big idea you're trying to get across. Get rid of the facts, the minutiae, the noise. What's the one take-home message? This is often lost. There's a tendency among science educators to get bogged down in facts and small details. These can often be irrelevant or confusing to the concept or skill at the heart of the lesson.

Step 2: Hook your audience

Ideally, students should be able to relate to the big idea from a personal perspective. For example, plate tectonics is one of geology's big ideas, but how do you make this concept relevant to students? Ask them if they've ever lived on the west coast of Canada, or if they know anyone who lives there. Explain how you love the west coast, but that you wouldn't live just anywhere. The west coast is tectonically active and therefore earthquake prone, so you'd look for ways to minimize the risk. You'd make sure your house was built on a solid bedrock, for example, be aware of the historical seismic activity in the area, and use science to assess the risk. If you are teaching a big idea like plate tectonics, make it relevant to the students' daily lives. There is always a way.

Step 3: Remember that you are not teaching to a blank slate

Take the time to figure out what the students already think about the big idea. I find that my students have their own notions about the planet and how it works, based on their experiences. For example, students who grew up on a farm have had a different experience with the natural world than those who grew up in a city. Or near an ocean. Or in another country. Teaching should be informed by the ideas students already have. If their ideas differ from the scientific explanations of the natural world, then these ideas should be addressed.

Here's one example. A student was asked "Do you think the Earth gets hotter or colder as you go deeper?" The student said colder. Why? Because she had been to Carlsbad Caverns in New Mexico and noticed it was colder in the cave, about 200 metres below the surface. As someone who teaches introductory geology, it's important for me to understand what students think about the planet and why. The Earth actually gets hotter with increasing depth, but I use this common misunderstanding as a jumping-off point for discussion.

If you don't understand the model that students come in with, you run the risk that they may just take the new information and pack it around those existing, incorrect models.

Step 4: Look to the end

How are you going to know if students learn something? Your decision about how to assess student learning will shape the kinds of activities you choose, so think carefully about how you are going to test students and assess their knowledge.

When you think about the questions you are planning to ask, you may find that they are not related to the big idea after all. Were you going to ask about facts? The minutiae?

Once you know how you will test the students to see if they understand the big idea, then—and only then—can plan some activities.

Step 5: Consider your activities carefully

This is the thing we tend to jump to first. In fact, it should be last.

I catch myself doing this. I get an activity all planned out. I get very excited and attached to it. This is normal—activities are fun, as is the interaction with the students. But you need to remember to take a step back and ask yourself: Have I picked the right instructional activity? One that allows me to assess whether or not students have learned the big idea? One that challenges them to reflect on their own ideas, and why they think that way?

The other thing with assessment is that, ideally, we want to be giving students constant feedback on their understanding throughout the course. This is where the challenge of big classes come in. How can meaningful feedback be given to so many students? I use learning (feedback) assessments in one of my courses. This is a way to give students an opportunity to see how their thinking has changed on five big ideas in geology over the semester.

Step 6: Be patient, start small

We know what the ingredients are for the ultimate science lesson plan, but sometimes circumstances don't allow us to teach that way. Personally, I find I don't always have the resources or the time (or the courage) to teach the way I want to teach. This can be frustrating. But be patient, tweak one thing at a time, assess how it worked, and go from there. There are so many challenges that we face in the classroom and every class is different. Rome wasn't built in a day, and neither is the ultimate science lesson plan.

The ultimate science lesson plan does all these things:

- Stays focused on a big idea

- Makes it relevant

- Understands the range of notions commonly held about this idea

- Knows how to assess whether the idea has been learned

- Uses the right activity

Ultimately all of these steps are student-centred; they don't have much to do with the instructor except in the planning stages.

The British Council is the U.K.'s international organiza-
tion for cultural relations. It runs hundreds of projects
supporting education, the arts, science, and sport.
In science, the Council focuses on the exchange of ideas
and knowledge about science and its impact upon society.
In April 2006, a group of British Council staff members
came up with an initiative called Beautiful Science, which
included a televised contest called FameLab, in which sci-
entists used creative approaches to present their scientific
ideas to the public. The concept, scale, and execution of
FameLab offers a high-impact approach to engaging the
public in science, in this case in Europe. Lyubov Kostova,
head of Projects and Partnerships for the British Council in
Bulgaria, files this report with support from James Morrison,
freelance journalist reporting on FameLab International
2009.

FameLab

Lyubov Kostova

How do you find new voices in science and engineering, new spokespersons for engaging the public in science, when the science system itself does not reward public outreach? Why not invent a laboratory for public outreach?

FameLab is an initiative of the Cheltenham Science Festivals in the U.K. and the British Council in Europe that has had an unprecedented impact on public dialogue about science. In fact, working through the media and other partners in southeast Europe, FameLab was in part responsible for a major perceptual shift in the social impact of science. FameLab is a "pop idol" contest for scientists that was broadcast, in part, on live TV and was aimed at an adult, non-scientific audience. Taking place between September 2006 and December 2009 in Austria, Azerbaijan, Bulgaria, Croatia, Greece, Israel, Romania, Serbia, Turkey, and the U.K., the show reached an audience of millions.

The FameLab competition takes place in two main laps—national and international. In each participating country, the format is identical. First there are the auditions (or heats), held in as many cities as is appropriate to the country. Ten to a dozen finalists are selected and are then taken through a two-day master class. In the end, they reach the grand national final. After the initial success of the program in southeast Europe, new countries joined on to participate as well. FameLab Hong Kong took place in November 2009 while a number of other countries were lined up for 2010.

The mission of contestants is to deliver a highly charismatic, totally clear, and uncompromisingly scientifically correct performance that explains a science concept. The performance is recorded for the Web and television, and can last no more than three minutes. Participants are allowed to dance, sing, recite poetry, and bring their own props as long as they do not use PowerPoint presentations or the like, or forget that the goal is to communicate about science.

BELOW The FameLab Web site.

"Participants are allowed to dance, sing, recite poetry, and bring their own props as long as they do not use PowerPoint presentations or the like, or forget that the goal is to communicate about science."

After the national winners have been chosen, they all meet in the U.K. at the Cheltenham Science Festival. Here they compete with each other and the International FameLab Winner is chosen. Winners are selected by both a jury's vote and an audience vote. Serbian Mirko Djordjevic, a molecular-biology student at the University of Belgrade, won in 2009 after singing lyrics from a pop song and taking the imagined viewpoints of animals to bring his presentation on sexual selection to life. Some of the other finalists were Maja Maraskovic, a chemist from Croatia, who won the audience vote in 2009 for her pitch on free radicals and aging, and Lucia Aronica, an Italian molecular biologist representing Austria, who used flowers and the story of Dr. Jekyll and Mr. Hyde to teach the audience about ribonucleic acid (RNA). Serious stuff, as you can see!

The number of media hits the show received reveals the popular success of the program. FameLab has contributed directly to forty TV broadcasts via media partners and been referenced in another one hundred TV items and several hundred radio and newspaper articles. Potential TV reach for FameLab is approaching fifty million across the region with thirty-three million potential viewers in Turkey alone. The young scientists who participate on the show often become media celebrities and receive VIP treatment wherever they go. Marko Kosicek from Croatia, for example, was profiled in *Cosmopolitan* and featured in crossword puzzles. Deniz Demiryurek of Turkey has dined in restaurants where owners have refused to take his money. Deniz and his fellow Turkish FameLabbers have also been introduced to royalty, performing versions of their competition entries for the Queen and British Foreign Secretary David Miliband on a British state visit to Istanbul. In Bulgaria, a finalist specializing in meteorology appeared on a popular cooking show explaining the links between alcoholic drinks and the Earth's atmosphere.

FameLab really did create fame for many young scientists, particularly in the Balkan countries, and is a fabulously successful lab experiment in two ways: it helps train young scientists to communicate more effectively, and it helps promulgate an interest in science. But words alone do not do justice to FameLab performances. Readers of this article should watch the show for themselves on YouTube, VBox7, or at FameLab.org.

As a direct result of FameLab's popularity, a number of young, highly skilled researchers, who were inspired by the multidisciplinary approaches to communication they saw on the show, were brought together to create an international network. In October 2009, the British Council brought together 150 scientists from across southeast Europe and the U.K. in Istanbul in order to help them develop their skills further and kick-start cross-border science communication projects. The event in Istanbul culminated in the Istanbul Declaration, a call to the science community within southeast Europe and the U.K. to support science communication and the existing network.

There are already signs that the work of successful FameLab candidates will be more enduring and influential than that of their aspiring pop-star counterparts. The 2007 Croatian winner, Fran Supek, used cell research to develop a revolutionary protein-printing procedure that has the potential to diagnose diseases earlier in plants and animals. His breakthrough earned him the annual State Award for Science from his country's Ministry of Science, Education, and Sport. Bozhidar Stefanov, a FameLab contestant in both 2007 and 2008, is now science reporter on the English-language *Sofia Echo*.

Most participants have gone on to use their experience on FameLab for the purpose it was created: to promote science communication. Spiros Kitsinelis, Greek 2007 champion, teamed up with fellow contestants to stage a variety of performances designed to capture the imaginations of children (and adult refuseniks) by relating science to human emotions and the world of make-believe. December 2007 saw *The Science of Christmas* staged in Thessalonica with young Greek FameLabbers using a combination of theatrical chutzpah and hard science to answer questions on such heavyweight topics as why Santa is fat. Valentine's Day 2009 in Athens witnessed the spectacle of Marko and fellow FameLab alumni from Britain, Israel, and Greece explaining the scientific basis of human relationships in a show entitled *The Science of Love*.

In Serbia, FameLab's impact has been more profound still, leading to the establishment of Belgrade's new annual scientific showcase, Festival Nauke.

But perhaps the last word on FameLab should go to a former international finalist, whose life was transformed by the program. For Deniz Demiryurek, thirty-nine, who is now an associate professor of anatomy at Hacettepe University and writing a children's book, FameLab is more than an entry on his CV; it's a personal crusade: "Science is everywhere in our lives. What FameLab does is open it to the public."

NOTE   At the time of publishing, Cheltenham Festivals and British Council had signed an agreement granting the latter licence to run FameLab competitions based on the original model in twenty countries in Europe, Asia, Africa, and South America. The International FameLab Final takes place during the Cheltenham Science Festival.

Film Crew

Jorge Cham

WWW.PHDCOMICS.COM

Many Hollywood films draw on the expertise of people in the science world in order to lend a degree of scientific authenticity to the stories—trying to employ some realistic classical physics, for example, while concocting a fantastically implausible journey through space. Adam Summers was the science consultant on Finding Nemo, and talks about his role on that film. As he explains, it takes a special suspension of disbelief to debate the anatomical correctness of fish that can talk. Adam is an associate professor at Friday Harbor Laboratories at the University of Washington and a contributor to Natural History magazine.

The Pixar Years

Adam Summers

Berkeley around the millennium was not the best place for a post-doc to look for housing. Prices were insanely high and my wife and I could only afford four hundred square feet in the basement of a house. We kept our hiking boots in storage because there was not room in the house for more than two pairs of shoes each. It was, nevertheless, a magical time, I was on fire with science, working at the best place in the country for plying my unusual trade, and through an amazing stroke of luck I had the opportunity to work with the overwhelmingly creative and enthusiastic people at Pixar Studios.

My landlady, Elyse Klaidman, worked at Pixar coordinating the internal education program that is one of the many unusual features of this most original company. Her job was to set up classes for people who wanted to learn things, sometimes technical, sometimes artistic, and at various size scales. As an aside she would dig up experts in various subjects when the creative folks wanted information about things in a more efficient and deeper sense than can be easily apprehended from books.

I am a biologist. That is, my doctorate is in biology. My undergraduate degrees are in mathematics and engineering, but I never worked at either after college. Instead, I apply the tools of these disciplines to living organisms. They too have to live in the world of Newton and Faraday, so there are things to be learned about biology looking through the lenses of these distant fields. I am a comparative biomechanist and I have worked on fishes, reptiles, and amphibians to try to understand the evolution and function of the systems that allow them to move, eat, mate, breathe, and grow.

This expertise is what brought Elyse to my door one evening with a strange request. Did I know anyone who could tell the folks at Pixar about how large animals move? It turned out that at Berkeley at that time there was the world's expert on that very topic. Rodger Kram cares about how elephants and hippos run, how we would walk on planets with more (or less gravity), and other locomotor conundrums. More importantly, he is a gifted communicator who can make the math-heavy world of Froude numbers, inertia, and momentum completely accessible. I gave Elyse his contact information and thought no more about it. Pixar quietly recruited Rodger to help them with the current project and some time later the characters of *Monsters, Inc.* showed how deeply they had internalized the lessons he taught them in lecture and his lab.

192

ABOVE Frame grab from the animated movie, *Finding Nemo*. Courtesy Pixar.

"I had no idea the exalted company that was gathered in the room, but in retrospect there were almost exactly as many Oscars on their mantelpieces as there were audience members."

Some time after this first successful talent search, Elyse again appeared at my door and asked if I knew anyone who could tell the Pixar gang about fish. When I asked what she needed to know she said "everything." When I asked why, she told me she could not say. I had enough ego to admit that fish were my passion and that I would be glad to help in any way I could … but please, would I get paid? The answer was yes, an hourly consulting fee. That sounded great since my wife and I were not unaware that we were living in what is arguably the restaurant capital of the free world. My first job, after signing a thick non-disclosure agreement, was to give an hour-long talk about fish to eight or ten people in a cavernous theatre at the Pixar campus in Richmond.

At this point I was quite a naive fellow; I had not seen an animated movie, we didn't (and still don't) own a television, and I'd had only heard of Pixar through wonderful short animations that periodically showed up at SIGGRAPH conferences and trickled out to a broader academic audience. I had no idea the exalted company that was gathered in the room, but in retrospect there were almost exactly as many Oscars on their mantelpieces as there were audience members. And, by the time the post-release Oscars rolled around, the few without a statue would have one.

I had no real plan for my lecture because I was given no guidance on the topic. "Just talk about fish" was my brief, and frankly that is an easy one for me. Give me a time frame and I can fill it with fish stories. I have always been fascinated by them and obsessed with their diversity, habits, and shape. I started putting up slides, waving my arms, and talking to my scattered audience about the creatures I had been studying hard for the past eight years. I was not five minutes in when the first questions started getting called out. Good questions, questions that made me think and also made me realize that this audience was both listening and processing what I was saying. I have often been asked what lecturing to the Pixar folks was like, and I liken it to teaching the most eager and excited graduate seminar. I wrapped up my hour talk, with about half the slides to go, in just under two hours. It was a great time and I thought to myself that I would be very happy to do something like that again.

Several days later Elyse came over and offered me a continuing job as a consultant on this still somewhat mysterious movie project. I spent the next twenty months or so acting as an advisor on what was to become the Oscar-winning movie *Finding*

BELOW Frame grab from the animated movie, *Finding Nemo*. Courtesy Pixar.

Nemo. I wore several hats: I was a direct source for information on fishes; I took various artists, writers, and technical wizards on field trips; and perhaps most importantly, I acted as a scientific pimp, arranging for my colleagues to give authoritative talks to the Pixar team. As a primary source, I taught a graduate-level course in ichthyology complete with labs and visits to aquariums and museums. They taped my lectures and as the personnel on the project changed, new folks would watch old lectures and then look me up to clarify or amplify certain points. Everyone on the *Nemo* team also had my email address and I would field specific questions, and they were often quite abstruse, on an ad hoc basis.

The experience with Pixar was at complete odds with many of my other interactions with the popular media. The folks at Pixar did not feel like the science was a barrier or a burden, but rather a joyful jumping off point for the story. I was always impressed by their willingness to rewrite, redraw, and rethink parts of the movie based on new facts. One day I was talking about fish sex, and fish sex is a very odd and diverse topic. I explained that male anglerfish live in the dark, abyssal depths and have a hard time finding mates, so when they do find one they latch on with their teeth. Eventually the female's flesh grows into the male's mouth and he becomes an appendage, a "testicular parasite" ready to deliver sperm when the need arises. My audience was just fascinated and it was no huge surprise when the light providing anglerfish in the movie ended up with a little parasitic male.

The leadership on the movie was also willing to spend real money to be scientifically accurate. One of the talks I arranged was from an expert on algae, Mike Graham from Moss Landing Marine Labs. At the end of his lecture an audience member asked the question that was always asked of the visiting fireman: "What would be the worst thing you could see in a movie about fishes on the Great Barrier Reef?" Mike replied that the real sin would be to put kelp on the reef; it is not found there and it supports a diverse community of its own in colder waters. Ricky Nierva, the character guru on the movie, called from the back row "don't see the movie." At that point there was kelp all over the artistic markups and storyboards of the Great Barrier Reef. Several weeks later all the kelp was gone, and the only evidence that remains is that kelp and coral share the screen in the book *The Art of Finding Nemo*. They redid a lot of work in order to be scientifically correct and my later experiences with the entertainment business make it clear how very rare this attitude is.

It could be argued that scientific accuracy is irrelevant in an animated story about an overprotective father and a young organism coming into his own. I could not disagree more and am overjoyed to have been associated with a group who firmly believed that a sound factual basis lent gravitas to the story. That is not to say there are not scientific errors. There are sharks without claspers, a hammerhead with misplaced nostrils, saltwater fish leaping harmlessly into fresh water, and whales

with a connection between the mouth and blowhole. There is even a sex error, as observed by one crusty old ichthyologist at a scientific meeting: clownfish live in a female-dominated social system. If the dominant female is removed, the most dominant male will immediately begin to transform in to a female. This means that midway through the trip to Sydney, Marlin should have become Marlene, a situation that no one but Dory would have appreciated. In the end, science was sometimes sacrificed on the altar of storytelling, but it was always done with a clear understanding of the science that was being tossed aside. As Ricky would say to me when I got particularly heated up about a lie in the world of fishes: "Calm down, fishes don't talk. It will be a bad movie if the fishes don't talk."

ABOVE Frame grab from the animated movie, *Finding Nemo*. Courtesy Pixar.

"In the end, science was sometimes sacrificed on the altar of storytelling, but it was always done with a clear understanding of the science that was being tossed aside."

Permissions

"The Value of Science," by Richard P. Feynman
Reprinted with permission from *What Do You Care What Other People Think?" Further Adventures of a Curious Character*, by Richard P. Feynman as told to Ralph Leighton. Copyright © 1988 by Gweneth Feynman and Ralph Leighton. Used by permission of W.W. Norton & Company, Inc.

"The Science News Cycle"
Jorge Cham © 2009
Reprinted with permission of the artist from www.phd comics.com

"Some Guidelines for Science Writers," by Alton Blakeslee and Sandra Blakeslee
Submitted for this volume by Sandra Blakeslee

"Research Topics for Media," "If TV Science Was More Like Real Science," "Great Tweets of Science," and "Film Crew 1-7"
Jorge Cham © 2009
Reprinted with permission of the artist from www.phd comics.com

"The Evolution of an Exhibit," by Pat Murphy
Excerpt reprinted with permission from "The Evolution of Exhibits" by Pat Murphy, *Working Prototypes* (San Francisco: Exploratorium, www.exploratorium.edu).

"Statement of Art and Science," by Billy Klüver
Billy Klüver © 2001 Berkeley Heights, New Jersey
Reprinted with permission from Julie Martin

"Godfather of Technology and Art: An Interview with Billy Klüver"
Interview April 19, 1995.
Reprinted with permission from Garnet Hertz

Kelly-Marie Murphy, "Dark Energy"
Copyright 2009 by Friedrich Hofmeister Musikverlag, Leipzig

"How to Start a Science Café"
Reprinted with permission from www.sciencecafes.org

Acknowledgements

Thank you to all of my collaborators at The Banff Centre, an extraordinary place for creativity, and an international jewel. I am especially grateful to Carol Holmes, who was the director of literary arts when I first approached the centre in 2003 with an idea. It was her attitude and support that enabled the creation of the Banff Science Communications Program. We launched in the fall of 2005, and have worked with a number of teams at The Banff Centre to deliver the program since then. It is a joy to be at the centre and we are grateful for the support of the many people involved. I can't think of another place in the world with such a magical combination of striking natural beauty, fabulous technology resources, and a commitment to creativity. Special thanks are due to The Banff Centre Press for taking on this book project on top of the program itself. Steven Ross Smith, Nick Hutcheson, and Janice Zawerbny have all played important roles and I gratefully acknowledge their support.

I am filled with thanks for the faculty members in the Banff Science Communications program who have poured their hearts and souls into creative science communications. You are the inspiration for this book. In some cases, you are also the authors of this book! There are so many people who have enriched the program in critical and enduring ways: musicians, scientists, artists, educators, designers, photographers, and, yes, some amazing external relations people in government. I need to mention a few people by name who have invested long periods of time in Banff: Thomas Hayden, Henry Kowalski, Jane Mingay, Christie Nicholson, Mark Winston, Erika Check Hayden—you have been with Jay and me, shoulder to shoulder (often dancing) for many weeks over the years, and your ideas and friendship mean a great deal to me personally and to the success of the program.

I also want to thank Elizabeth Cannon, Suzanne Corbeil, and Blair Dickerson for their key support roles. We are grateful to the individuals like these in research-related organizations who understand that communications is the last step of doing science, not an add-on. Randy Goebel and Sho Sengupta at the Alberta Informatics Circle of Research Excellence (now Alberta Innovates) have been long-time supporters, and we have always enjoyed our partnership with them.

Thank you also to the participants in the Banff Science Communications program. The circle of people I treasure and trust grows wider every year with the rather amazing individuals we get to know through this program.

Thank you to Wendy for leading me on so many childhood adventures that animated the natural world. That's where I fell in love with science.

Thank you to my family, especially my teenage children, Grace, Jasper, and Finn, who showed me that it's okay to say you love this and love that so freely.

Finally, thank you to Jay—for his love, and his love of science.

About the Contributors

Editor

Mary Anne Moser works at the crossroads of research, culture, and communications. She holds a bachelor of science degree in zoology, a master of arts degree in communications, and an interdisciplinary Ph.D. concerning the application of technology in everyday life. She was co-editor of *Immersed in Technology: Art and Virtual Environments*, published by MIT Press, and founding editor of The Banff Centre Press. She is also the founder and director of the Banff Science Communications program.

Contributors

Alton Blakeslee (1914–97) was a long-time science editor of The Associated Press and a regular contributor of science articles for the *New York Times*.

Sandra Blakeslee is a writer for the *New York Times* and the author of several books.

Christian Bök is a Canadian experimental poet who teaches at the University of Calgary.

Jorge Cham is the writer and artist of *Piled Higher and Deeper*, a comic strip about life, or the lack thereof, in academia.

Duncan Dallas is a science communicator who started the Café Scientifique movement when he organized the first café in Leeds in the U.K. in 1998.

Tracy Day is an Emmy Award-winning documentary producer and co-founder of the World Science Festival in New York, along with her husband, Brian Green, a Columbia University physics professor, author, and broadcaster.

Richard P. Feynman (1918–88) received the Nobel Prize in Physics in 1965. He was a keen popularizer of physics in books and lectures and was known for his wide-ranging interests.

Garnet Hertz is a contemporary artist and Fulbright Scholar who explores themes of technological progress, creativity, innovation, and interdisciplinarity. He is a faculty member at the Art Center College of Design in Pasadena, California, and is artist-in-residence at University of California Irvine.

Jay Ingram is a science writer and broadcaster who has hosted a television show on Discovery Channel in Canada for fifteen years. He is the author of eleven popular books on science, and is chair of the Banff Science Communications program.

Billy Klüver (1927–2004) was an electrical engineer at Bell Telephone Laboratories and the founder of Experiments in Art and Technology.

Lyubov Kostova is Head, Projects and Partnerships, for the British Council in Bulgaria, and Regional Manager, Beautiful Science, in southeast Europe.

Lawrence M. Krauss is a professor in the physics department and director of the Origins Initiative at Arizona State University. He is the author of several best-selling books, including *The Physics of Star Trek*.

Roger Malina is an astrophysicist at the Laboratoire d'Astrophysique de Marseille CNRS in France and executive editor of the Leonardo publications at MIT Press, including the Leonardo Book Series and Journals.

Julie Martin is the wife of Billy Klüver, and worked with him and E.A.T. since 1968.

Kelly-Marie Murphy is an award-winning Canadian composer whose extraordinary work has been performed and broadcast around the world.

Pat Murphy is a science fiction writer and long-time science writer, specializing in science and photography books for the Exploratorium in San Francisco.

Christie Nicholson is a freelance science journalist in New York. She hosts and produces the weekly audio podcast *60-Second Mind*, and is an online contributor at *Scientific American*.

Leslie Reid holds the Tamaratt Teaching Professorship in Geoscience at the University of Calgary in Alberta, Canada.

Rosalind Reid is director of the Initiative in Innovative Computing at Harvard University. She was the editor of *American Scientist* from 1992 to 2008.

Susan Schwartzenberg and Shawn Lani are senior artists who hold long-term staff positions at the Exploratorium in San Francisco. They are responsible for program and exhibit development and are curators of two new exhibit environments currently planned for the Exploratorium.

Simon Singh holds a Ph.D. in physics and is the author of several books and numerous television and radio broadcasts that popularize science. He is a frequent presenter and commentator on science and lives in the U.K.

Frankie Solarik is the owner of Barchef in Toronto, Ontario. He has created an almost culinary drink experience with his passion for cocktails that inspire all of the senses. (See www.barcheftoronto.com.)

Adam Summers is an associate professor at Friday Harbor Laboratories at the University of Washington and a contributor to *Natural History* magazine.

John Swain is an experimental high-energy physicist with a strong interest in related theory at Northeastern University in Boston. He is also a frequent contributor to texts and broadcasts aimed at general audiences.

Index